W. E. B. Du BOIS

AVAILABLE UP CLOSE TITLES:

RACHEL CARSON by Ellen Levine

JOHNNY CASH by Anne E. Neimark

W. E. B. DU BOIS by Tonya Bolden

ELLA FITZGERALD by Tanya Lee Stone

BILL GATES by Marc Aronson

JANE GOODALL by Sudipta Bardhan-Quallen

ROBERT F. KENNEDY by Marc Aronson

THURGOOD MARSHALL by Chris Crowe

ELVIS PRESLEY by Wilborn Hampton

RONALD REAGAN by James Sutherland

JOHN STEINBECK by Milton Meltzer

OPRAH WINFREY by Ilene Cooper

FRANK LLOYD WRIGHT by Jan Adkins

FUTURE UP CLOSE TITLES:

HARPER LEE by Kerry Madden

THEODORE ROOSEVELT by Michael Cooper

BABE RUTH by Wilborn Hampton

UPclose:

W. E. B. Du BOIS

a twentieth-century life by
TONYA BOLDEN

VIKING

For

Cousin Jordan William Freeland

VIKING

Published by Penguin Group

Penguin Young Readers Group, 345 Hudson Street, New York, New York 10014, U.S.A.

Penguin Group (Canada), 90 Eglinton Avenue East, Suite 700, Toronto, Ontario,
Canada M4P 2Y3 (a division of Pearson Penguin Canada Inc.)

Penguin Books Ltd, 80 Strand, London WC2R 0RL, England

Penguin Ireland, 25 St Stephen's Green, Dublin 2, Ireland (a division of Penguin Books Ltd)

Penguin Group (Australia), 250 Camberwell Road, Camberwell, Victoria 3124, Australia
(a division of Pearson Australia Group Pty Ltd)

Penguin Books India Pvt Ltd, 11 Community Centre, Panchsheel Park, New Delhi – 110 017, India

Penguin Group (NZ), 67 Apollo Drive, Rosedale, North Shore 0632, New Zealand
(a division of Pearson New Zealand Ltd)

Penguin Books (South Africa) (Pty) Ltd, 24 Sturdee Avenue, Rosebank, Johannesburg 2196,
South Africa

Penguin Books Ltd, Registered Offices: 80 Strand, London WC2R 0RL, England

First published in 2008 by Viking, a division of Penguin Young Readers Group

10 9 8 7 6 5 4 3 2 1

LIBRARY OF CONGRESS CATALOGING-IN-PUBLICATION DATA

Bolden, Tonya.

Up close, W.E.B. Du Bois : a twentieth-century life / by Tonya Bolden.

p. cm.

Includes bibliographical references and index.

ISBN 978-0-670-06302-4 (hardcover) 1. Du Bois, W. E. B. (William Edward Burghardt),
1868–1963—Juvenile literature. 2. African Americans—Biography—Juvenile literature.
3. African American intellectuals—Biography—Juvenile literature. 4. African American civil
rights workers—Biography—Juvenile literature. I. Title.

E185.97.D73B54 2008

303.48'4092—dc22

[B]

2007052380

Printed in the U.S.A.   Set in Goudy   Book design by Jim Hoover

ACKNOWLEDGMENTS

So grateful to my Viking editor, Anne Gunton, for your curiosity, exuberance, and the terrific back-and-forth.

Executive Production Editor, Janet Pascal—you are just too sharp. Nicolas Medina—bless your eagle eyes and skills. Designer Jim Hoover—love your vision. Publisher Regina Hayes—many thanks for saying yes to Du Bois in the first place.

For your gracious and speedy responses to my inquiries, long and short, thank you so much, Beth Madison Howse, Librarian, Special Collections, John Hope and Aurelia Elizabeth Franklin Library, Fisk University, and Danielle Kovacs, Curator of Manuscripts and University Archives, Special Collections and University Archives, W. E. B. Du Bois Library, University of Massachusetts Amherst.

For your careful reading of the last draft, the critique, and the contending with all my questions, I can't thank you enough, Dr. Daryl Michael Scott, Howard University, Professor of History and Vice President of the Association for the Study of African American Life and History.

For the strength to strive with the incomparable W. E. B. Du Bois, I have to thank God.

CONTENTS

The pronunciation of my name is *Due Boyss*, with the accent on the last syllable.

—W. E. B. Du Bois, January 20, 1939

FOREWORD

I HAVE BEEN CAPTIVATED by the bold, boundless Du Bois for years: now worshipful, now annoyed with him, sometimes merely perplexed. Always astonished.

He did so much, this titanic talent in a small body, this David challenging Goliaths, this dreamer and realist and sometimes elitist, this man of intellect and soul. For decades, through words and in other ways, Du Bois battled mightily for a righteous America—a righteous world—daring to dream that life on earth could be heavenly.

For all.

I like that kind of energy. I need that kind of energy. The dreamer in me longs to see it in superabundance today.

That's why I wrote this book, hoping that you, the reader, will be guided by the spirit of Du Bois's life.

Berlin, Germany, Oranienstrasse N° 130 A.

PROGRAM
for the

Celebration of my twenty-fifth birth day

Birth day - eve.

7 – 9 – Music.   10½ – 12 letters to { Grandma, Mabel, ~~Emma~~

9 – 10½ – Plans   12. Sacrifice to the Zeitgeist
(Mercy – God – work)

Birth day.

7 – 8 – 9½ : Breakfast - old letter   6 – 7   Seminar
Reflection { Parents, Home   Mem'lo   7 – 8 .   Supper { Greek wine, Cocoa, Kuchen, Oranges
Poetry ——
Song { Steal Away, Jesus lover of my soul, Amerika   8 – 10 · Year book

9½ – 11. A Wander.   10 – 12 letters to { C.B. Carrington, ~~Mrs Green~~, Florence, ~~Fell~~, A Smith, ~~Refenbum~~?, ~~Hart~~, ~~Herald~~

11 – 1. Art.

1 – 3 Dinner

3 – 6 Coffee in Potsdam

W.E.D. Du Bois.

INTRODUCTION

"O I WONDER what I am—I wonder what the world is—I wonder if Life is worth the striving."

It's around midnight. Du Bois wonders on paper in a rented room worlds away from home, after a string of successes.

If only his mother could see him now.

Her son is now a man.

Her son, restless, reflects on his life and tries to fathom his future on his twenty-fifth birthday, February 23, 1893.

As a boy, a "great bitterness entered" his life and "kindled a great ambition." Back then he wondered, *Will I make a name for myself as a lawyer? A doctor?*

As his birthday program shows, Du Bois was truly into time management.

Or "by telling the wonderful tales that swam in my head"?

Could *one* thing satisfy his energies and the constant questing?

On this night, the churning, yearning young man decides that life *is* worth the striving. He aims at ambitions greater than anything he imagined as a boy.

ONE

"DEAR MAM,

I arrived here safely friday after noon."

July 21, 1883.

"Mam" was Du Bois's mother, Mary.

"Here," the Bay State whaling town of New Bedford, almost two hundred miles east of their village, Great Barrington, Massachusetts.

This trip, which he later called his "first great excursion into the world," included a layover in Hartford, Connecticut, where he polished off his packed lunch, purchased a ticket for his next train, and still had time to kill. Instead of staring at railroad tracks, he checked out the statehouse in nearby Bushnell Park.

Mam got a tour: "The grounds are laid out beautifully and the building is magnificent." Once inside, with the frescoes, flags, and marble floors, he didn't overlook the guest book: "& of course my illustrious name is there."

William Edward Du Bois—but Willie is what most folks called this fifteen-year-old boy so devoted to his mother.

Several years before Willie was born, Dear Mam had a love affair that ended with her pregnant, but unmarried—grounds for being shunned in some families. Mary's parents, Othello and Sarah Burghardt, weren't like that. They helped her raise the baby, a boy named Adelbert, born in 1862.

The Burghardts lived a little ways west of Great Barrington on Egremont Plain. Their American heritage began in the 1700s with a young West African called Tom by those who held him in slavery. The last person to own him was Conrad Burghardt, a Dutchman with lots of land in the area.

Burghardt's Tom became Tom Burghardt after he was freed for service in the Revolutionary War, it seems. By thrift or gift, he also had land to farm on

Baby Du Bois with his "Mam."

Egremont Plain. Some of this land fell to grandson Othello, who had a passel of kids with wife Sarah (of African and Dutch decent). Willie's mother, Mary, was their youngest.

After Mary had Adelbert, she didn't swear off men during her days of drudgery as a domestic worker in Great Barrington. One day she fell for a stranger to the village: Alfred Du Bois, a sometime waiter, barber, and baker.

Something about Alfred made the Burghardts uneasy, but Mary followed her bliss and eloped. The lovebirds married in nearby Housatonic in early February 1867. Willie was born a year later, on Sunday, February 23, 1868.

This was a few years after the Civil War, during Reconstruction. The Republican Party, "the party of Abraham Lincoln" and largely of the North, had a band of whites on fire for blacks to have the same rights as whites. These Radical Republicans also championed schools and other social services for the roughly four million children and adults shaking loose slavery.

The majority of blacks lived in the South, where there were frequent white-on-black massacres because most white Southerners (largely Democrats) were hell-bent on white rule. (The Democratic Party wouldn't become associated with black civil rights until the late twentieth century.)

Rabidly racist whites had a strong ally in Lincoln's successor, Andrew Johnson. He despised black people. His opposition to pro-black initiatives had a lot to do with the Radical Republicans' fever to impeach him. That happened on February 24, 1868, the day after Willie was born.

Blacks thought, *Rats!* when President Johnson was acquitted of the impeachment charges in May. It was Johnson's turn to rage two months later when the Fourteenth Amendment became law. Now blacks, along with other people born or naturalized in the U.S., were citizens. White-on-black violence increased.

Overwhelmingly white Great Barrington, at the foot of the Berkshire Mountains, was not prejudice-free. Neither did it roil with racial strife. The black community was tiny. Plus, most whites there were Republicans.

Most Great Barrington blacks were go-along-to-get-along folks, working service jobs (maids, cooks, porters) or as laborers and small farmers. Some, like "Old Jeff," were very enterprising. He was a coach-man for a white family, peddled produce that sprang from his own ground, and dabbled in real estate. One property Old Jeff owned was a cozy house on Church Street. This was Willie's first home, but not for long.

When he was going on two, his father left. Willie and his mother soon joined Adelbert on Egremont Plain, in Othello and Sarah Burghardt's two-story house with a mighty elm out front. Up one hill, lived Othello's brother Ira; down another hill, brother Harlow in a little red house with secret passages.

Willie's standout memory of his days on Egremont Plain was not of any secret-passage adventures with Adelbert, but rather a haunting bit of family history told around his grandparents' fireside. There once was a female ancestor prone to croon an African tune that began, "Do bana coba, gene me, gene me!"

That's how grown-up Willie would transliterate these words. He never landed a translation and never had a clue as to exactly whence this woman came, but the song, he knew, was a soul-cry of discontent: a longing for her African way of life lost.

✳ ✳ ✳

Alfred Du Bois wasn't the only loss young Willie suffered. By the time he was eleven, his grandparents were dead and their homeplace in other hands due to debt. Willie lived in wretched rentals in Great Barrington from about age five. One was a rundown house on Railroad Street shared with a destitute white family.

Money got tighter after Willie's mother had a stroke, which left her weak and weary. She may have had a withered arm, leg, or both. Over the years, her son would give conflicting information about her infirmity. For sure, Mary continued to work—had to—but was limited to things like mending clothes and light housekeeping. Some Burghardts contributed food, clothing, and coin to Mary and Willie's keep. Adelbert, working up in Albany, sometimes sent money.

Over the years, Willie, short and scrawny, chopped wood for neighbors; mowed lawns; ran errands; delivered a white-owned daily newspaper, Massachusetts's *Springfield Republican*; and sold subscriptions to the black-owned *New York Globe* (a weekly). He played as hard as he worked, from mountain hiking to sledding down snow-packed hills. School, however, was where this leftie's life shone brightest.

There was a Mike who bested him at marbles, but not in Latin.

Redhead Art was an excellent visual artist, but Willie a better writer. When the two teamed up on a high-school newspaper, the short-lived *Howler*, Willie handled the copy, and Art, the illustrations.

From elementary school through high school, Willie especially stood out. On top of being a stellar student, he was the only black in his class or school for most of his youth. With relatively few Americans attending college back then and many people thinking blacks unfit for it, Willie's high-school principal, Frank Hosmer, had put him on the college track.

Bookshop owner Johnny Morgan was another white man who smiled on this boy's quick and hungry mind. Morgan's wares were Willie's window onto the world. In books and periodicals, he first saw pictures of famous Americans like President Ulysses S. Grant, elected when Willie was a baby. During this Republican's two terms in office, black men gained the national vote through the Fifteenth Amendment (1870). Also a civil-rights act (1875) outlawed racial discrimination in public facilities, such as trains. What's more, Grant tried to stamp out the KKK and other white supremacist groups, which bullied, beat, and killed blacks who exercised their rights and whites who supported them.

The next president, Rutherford B. Hayes, was also a Republican, but he didn't much care what happened to blacks. Willie first saw Hayes's likeness in Morgan's store, where he hung out as much as he pleased, reading things he couldn't afford to buy, and ever fascinated with the very *look* of books.

One day, Willie saw a must-have: a fancy edition of Thomas Babington Macaulay's five-volume *The History of England*. Morgan let him buy the set on a layaway plan (twenty-five-cents a week). Those tomes were in Willie's home by Christmas. By now, home wasn't on Railroad Street but back on Church Street near the rear of First Congregational Church. Willie and his mother were its only black members.

Mary Du Bois hoped for a rise in her son's fortunes in 1883 when a letter arrived from New Bedford. The sender was Annie Du Bois, the latest wife of Alexander Du Bois, Willie's paternal grandfather. Though she was not Alfred's mother, Annie thought her husband, Alfred's father, now in his eighties, should see this grandson before he died.

Plans were made for Willie to visit New Bedford.

"The railroad runs down parelal with the Connecticut river & the scenery is beautiful," he wrote Dear Mam, savoring his sightings of sailboats, steamships, and seaside resorts during the ride to Providence, Rhode Island, where he was to stay overnight with Burghardt kin and "went around a good deal what little time I was there." The next morning, the young traveler boarded an eight o'clock train to New Bedford. Three hours later, he was at 93 Acushnet Avenue, a white house with green shutters.

Grandma Annie was warm and cheery. Willie liked her a lot, his mother learned. Liking Grandpa Alexander—not so easy. This short, stocky, white-looking man was a cold-heart. Grandma Annie assured Willie that his grandfather would open up in time.

Didn't happen. He apparently told Willie zilch about Alfred, nor about his own miserable beginnings.

Alexander's father was James Du Bois, a white doctor of French descent from Poughkeepsie, New York, who had plantations in Haiti and on the Bahama islands. Dr. Du Bois sired several children with an enslaved woman on the island of Long Cay. Around 1812, he brought sons Alexander and John to the U.S. and sent them to a private school in Connecticut, ready to raise them as white. With his sudden death, the boys were once again "colored" or "Negro" as blacks were commonly called. Their white relatives pulled them out of school and forced them to learn a trade. Alexander, apprenticed to a shoemaker, ended up in business for himself. One enterprise was a grocery store in New Haven, Connecticut.

Still, Alexander Du Bois wanted more—like some of his father's property. That's why he went to Haiti at one point. He returned no richer, but had fathered at least one child, Willie's father. (When Alfred came to the U.S. is a mystery; so, too, is when Annie and Alexander Du Bois learned of Willie's whereabouts.)

When Willie stopped off in Providence on his way home, he joined relatives in a jaunt down to Narragansett Bay for an annual First of August cel-

ebration, commemorating August 1, 1834. That was
the day the abolition of slavery in the British Empire
went into effect, a date as hallowed to many blacks in
the U.S. as it was to black British subjects.

Thousands of people were at the First of August
festivities Willie witnessed. He was awed by the sight of
so many black folks "of every hue and bearing." He was
buoyed by "the swaggering men, the beautiful girls, the
laughter and gaiety, the unhampered self-expression."

After this, his village would feel even smaller.

TWO

"DURING MY TRIP—"

No, not another letter to his mother, but a snippet from his piece in a September 1883 issue of the *New York Globe*. Willie had been writing for the newspaper since April, for free—and happily so. The experience was worth more than money. Plus, he admired the "fierce brave voice" of the *Globe*'s militant editor in chief, T. Thomas Fortune. Tall, thin, high-strung, Fortune had been born into slavery in Marianna, Florida, and during Reconstruction the KKK had run his family out of town because of his father's activism.

Willie's voice was quite fierce when reporting on his trip in the *Globe*. He was "pleased to see the industry and wealth of many of our race," but irked by the "absence of literary societies" (think book clubs). "It seems to me as if this of all things ought not to be neglected," scolded Willie, whose pieces usually had the byline "W.E.D."

As a correspondent for the *Globe* (and its second act, the *New York Freeman*, beginning late 1884), Willie reported on a range of happenings, from births and deaths to the comings and goings of visitors and townsfolk. A leap-year ball and a trip to Lake Buel are among the special events he covered.

For church news, Willie spent the most ink on his town's African Methodist Episcopal (AME) Zion congregation, from its visiting preachers and its sewing-circle activities to debates it sponsored.

"Ought the Indian to have been driven out of America?" was one such debate in which Willie took part. There were only about 300,000 Native Americans left from sea to shining sea, with roughly 240,000 of them living on reservations.

"Should Indians be educated at Hampton?" was another debate. "Hampton" is today's Hampton University, in Hampton, Virginia. Back then, it was Hampton Normal and Agricultural Institute, a teacher-training and vocational school for blacks and Native Americans, founded after the Civil War.

We don't know which side Willie argued in the first debate about Native Americans, but in the second one: *Yes!*

He said *Oh Yes!* to blacks being involved in politics.

"I did not notice many colored men at the town meeting last month, it seems that they do not take as much interest in politics as is necessary for the protection of their rights," he tsked in his first *Globe* column.

In a later column: "The colored people here do not, as a whole, regard the proposed Colored Convention in a very favorable light." Willie was talking about the upcoming National Convention of Colored Men in Louisville, Kentucky's Liederkranz Hall in late September 1883. At the time, cases challenging the 1875 civil-rights act were before the U.S. Supreme Court.

The man who presided over that 1883 convention in Kentucky was sixty-five-year-old Frederick Douglass, who had spent the first twenty years of his life in slavery and after his escape became a leading abolitionist and civil-rights activist.

"Though we have had war, reconstruction, and abolition as a nation we still linger in the shadow and blight of an extinct institution [slavery]," Douglass stated in his address, a searing condemnation of the "color line" (racial discrimination).

Douglass longed for the day when a person's color would be a mere fact, not grounds for being kept down. Until then, blacks had to "keep their grievances before the people and make every organized protest against the wrongs inflicted upon them within their power."

Soon after the convention, the U.S. Supreme Court ruled that the civil-rights act was unconstitutional.

In an effort to combat black apathy in Great Barrington, Willie cofounded the Sons of Freedom and served as the first secretary and treasurer of this combined book club and consciousness-raising group. Early on, the Sons of Freedom undertook a study of U.S. history, as Willie reported.

By then, he had been in the news. A July 1884 issue of the *Globe* ran a letter congratulating "young Willie Du Bois, who has just graduated with high honors from the High School at Great Barrington."

The speech Willie gave on graduation day saluted the white radical Wendell Phillips, who had died

Great Barrington High's class of 1884. Seated center, Willie's mentor, Principal Frank Hosmer.

recently. Born into a wealthy Boston family and a graduate of Harvard College and Law School, Wendell Phillips hadn't let privilege dull him to the plight of others. Before the Civil War, he crusaded against slavery; after, for full citizenship rights for blacks and women. Phillips was also a socialist, believing that capitalism was at the root of many social ills (like poverty) because it can put profit above the good of people. Socialism calls for the opposite.

Willie knew little of Wendell Phillips the socialist.

Phillips the abolitionist was the focus of his speech, which garnered "repeated applause," according to the *Berkshire Courier*.

Dear Mam was beaming. Her son was Great Barrington High's first black and youngest graduate (sixteen)—and with high honors! He had an even greater ambition: Harvard College.

Quite a reach, yes, but aiming for the sun, the moon—the stars—was second nature. Never mind that he was poor. Never mind that this college created for wealthy white young men had admitted only a handful of blacks in its two-hundred-plus-year history. Harvard was considered the best, and the best is what Willie wanted.

But could he really leave Dear Mam?

That was not an issue after March 23, 1885, the day his mother died, leaving him in a tangle of grief and relief. His number-one fan was gone, but her suffering was over. So, too, his worry. He later described his clashing emotions as the "solemn feel of wings!"

About six months later, Willie was in college, but not at Harvard.

A group of white townsfolk that included Frank

Hosmer and Reverend Scudder, pastor of First Congregational, had devised a plan: Scudder's church and three other area churches would provide twenty-five dollars a year for Willie to attend a school founded by Congregationalists. The school was majority-black Fisk University in Nashville, Tennessee.

Willie winced at Fisk because his heart was still set on Harvard, but he wasn't a fool. Attending Fisk beat staying in Great Barrington.

The brainy boy headed South in late summer, 1885. Among the keepsakes he took along: a wrought-iron shovel and a pair of tongs, relics from Grandpa and Grandma Burghardt's fireside.

THREE

"OUR UNIVERSITY IS very pleasantly situated, overlooking the city," Willie wrote Reverend Scudder. Yes, the young scholar was having a fine time at Fisk, but "I have not forgotten to love my New England hills," he assured his benefactor. Willie had entered Fisk as a sophomore because his Up North education surpassed that of most young Southerners, and most Fisk students were Southerners.

For Willie, being at Fisk was like being at that First of August celebration. It was so exhilarating not to be a minority—and to be alive! Shortly after he started college, he was felled by typhoid fever.

Once back from the brink, Willie did well academically, from Greek, Latin, and German to philosophy and physics—and he relished that, as he did lending his voice (baritone) to Fisk's classical music choir, the Mozart Society. He didn't join, but he adored the Fisk Jubilee Singers, famous for their renditions of "Steal Away," "Swing Low, Sweet Chariot," and other spirituals: Bible-based songs of suffering and hope born in the souls of blacks in bondage.

Singing was a lark. Working on the school newspaper, the *Fisk Herald*—a passion. Senior year, Willie was editor in chief and not shy about publishing himself. His novella *Tom Brown at Fisk* was serialized in the *Herald* (winter 1887–1888).

This story about a country boy finding self-worth and a sweetheart at Fisk begins: "Oh, she was so tired! The long road stretched on and on until it was lost in the gathering twilight. It's hard to be a woman, but a black one,—!" This fictional young woman is feisty Fisk student Ella Boyd, seeking a temporary teaching post in rural Tennessee.

Willie had taught in the country for two summers, and had seen how hard it was to be a poor black person in the South, where, yearly, scores of blacks were lynched: murdered by a mob, whether hanged from a tree or killed in some other gruesome way. "Lynching was a continuing and recurrent horror during my college days," Willie later wrote. "Each death was a scar upon my soul." Whenever he left campus, he was careful and braced for racial insult.

The cabin in which he taught was an insult: backless benches, no door, few books. Some of his students were bright and eager. Others didn't even know they lived in Tennessee until he started teaching geography.

"For those who have the good of the race at heart this is an excellent field of work," he wrote in "The Hills of Tenn." for the *Fisk Herald*, where he constantly challenged fellow students to think and act *big*.

"Why isn't there a Fisk student at Leipzig, or a Fisk metaphysician at Berlin?" he asked in his April 1888 editorial. Weren't blacks smart enough for these grand German universities?

Two months later, on graduation day, Willie gave a speech on a German he idolized: Otto von Bismarck. By the early 1870s, mostly through warfare, this Prussian prime minister had wrangled more than thirty independent Germanic states into one nation, the German Empire. Bismarck, said Willie, was a prime example of "the power and purpose, the force of

Twenty-year-old Du Bois (seated left) with all but one of Fisk's Class of 1888.

an idea" and showed "what a man can do if he will."

By graduation day 1888, the will-powered young man from Great Barrington had made Burghardt part of his "illustrious name" and was signing letters "W. E. B. Du Bois." As historian David Levering Lewis put it: "Willie is no more."

✳ ✳ ✳

Fisk was chapter one in what W. E. B. Du Bois called his "Age of Miracles." Chapter two began in the fall of 1888, when he headed to Cambridge, Massachusetts, for a dream come true—Harvard!—and determined to earn a Ph.D.

His acceptance came with a scholarship, but like graduates of other colleges not in Harvard's league, Du Bois had to earn a Harvard bachelor's degree first. He entered as a junior.

And with his guard up.

"I sought no friendships among my white fellow students." This was his defense against being snubbed—likely even if he were white, because he was poor. (So was the other black in his class, chipper Clement Morgan.)

In any event, Du Bois was not at Harvard to make friends, but "to enlarge my grasp of the meaning of the universe." Over the next few years, he would knock himself out for his courses, from American and European history to Roman law, U.S. government, economics, and philosophy. He lived in the library. (He slept in a rented room at 20 Flagg Street.)

English was Du Bois's stumbling block at the out-set. "Words and ideas surged in my mind and spilled out with disregard of exact accuracy in grammar, taste in word or restraint in style." Result: a failing grade on his first English composition.

He had to do better. As he explained in an assign-ment, "I believe, foolishly perhaps but sincerely, that I have something to say to the world and I have taken English twelve in order to say it well."

October 1890.

By then he had earned his Harvard bachelor's de-gree in philosophy, with honors. Again, on graduation day, he had his say, as one of six commencement speak-ers in a class of close to three hundred, with Clement Morgan as class-day orator.

This time Du Bois spoke about a man he did not admire: Jefferson Davis, president of the Confederacy, and long before that, a soldier in wars against Native Americans and in the U.S.-Mexican War. Jefferson Davis, argued Du Bois, was a representative of a dan-gerous doctrine: "the advance of a part of the world at the expense of the whole."

Bravo! thought Henry Codman Potter, the Episcopal

Church's Bishop of New York. Reverend Potter's enthusiasm for Du Bois's address ran in the *Boston Herald*. As the cleric listened to the speech, he said to himself, *See what blacks can achieve "if they have a clear field, a high purpose, and a resolute will."*

Having fine professors helped. Du Bois's included philosopher William James (older brother of the novelist Henry James). Professor James was also a friend. As such, he advised Du Bois not to get his Ph.D. in philosophy because his options would be limited when it came to earning a living.

Du Bois would have gotten his Ph.D. in sociology if Harvard had had such a department. He was fascinated with what was then a new discipline exploring the ways of societies and social problems.

The U.S. had plenty of social problems. Du Bois's "Age of Miracles" coincided with the age of the robber barons, with careening corporate greed resulting in the enrichment of a few at the expense of the many: like factory workers pulling long hours in loathsome conditions for very low wages. Some workers resisted the abuse through strikes and by advocating socialism. Under socialism, all or key means of production (a factory for example) and what was produced would be managed by the government.

Capitalism prevailed. The rich got richer. The wretched abounded, as Jacob Riis captured in his 1890 book, *How the Other Half Lives*, about the cramped and crime-ridden lives of largely immigrant tenement dwellers on New York City's Lower East Side.

It's your fault! thought many of the well off, believing that people who didn't thrive were inferior. Blacks were considered the most inferior. This left white America with "the Negro Problem": What in the world are we to do with black folks in *our* nation?

For one, white lawmakers in majority-black Mississippi sabotaged black voting power by making men pay a poll tax (two dollars) and pass a literacy test in order to register to vote. This "Mississippi Plan," which also hurt some poor and illiterate whites but was more strictly enforced against blacks, became law in August 1890, a few months after Du Bois's speech on Jefferson Davis.

After considering economics, Du Bois decided to get his master's degree and Ph.D. in history. Now his chief mentor was Professor Albert Bushnell Hart, a real hound dog on history. Hart made his students forage far and wide for facts, by poring over primary documents from birth records and congressional records to census data, laws, and letters.

Du Bois would do a lot of that for his master's thesis. His topic: the slave trade.

Du Bois wasn't a total grind. Beyond Harvard, there was a sizeable black community, mostly in nearby Boston. He and Clement Morgan could enjoy boat rides on the Charles River, soirees, and Sunday dinners with their own. And, oh, yes, there were young ladies over whom Du Bois swooned. One was Deenie Pindell, but she gave her heart to another Harvard man, William Monroe Trotter—Monroe to friends and family.

A bicycle freak (and speed demon), Monroe Trotter entered Harvard College after Du Bois, in the fall of 1891. The two socialized together within the black community, but they weren't running buddies at Harvard. Trotter felt, as Du Bois put it, that black students "must not herd together."

Friendships with white students came easy for

Trotter. He had grown up in the mostly white Boston suburb of Hyde Park and his family had money.

Money was something Du Bois really wanted more of so he could live his new dream of studying abroad. He got his hopes up at a card party in late fall 1890, when a friend handed him a newspaper clipping. It was about a speech by former president Rutherford B. Hayes.

Hayes was head of the Slater Fund for Negro Education, created with an endowment of $1 million by the white industrialist John Fox Slater. In his speech, Hayes mentioned a Slater Fund initiative.

The good news: "If there is any young colored man in the South whom we find to have a talent for art or literature, or any especial aptitude for study," the Slater Fund would give that young man financial aid to study abroad or earn an advanced degree in the U.S.

The bad news: Hayes doubted there was a black who qualified.

"I am a Negro, twenty-three years of age next February," Du Bois informed Hayes in a November 1890 letter (apparently reasoning that his years at Fisk made him an honorary "colored man in the South.") Du

Bois went on to give his academic credentials, note that Harvard had given him several fellowships, and list ten distinguished men ready to provide references, starting with Harvard's president, Charles Eliot.

Hayes ended up telling Du Bois that the initiative had been scrapped.

Du Bois cried foul—fraud. "I think you owe an apology to the Negro people," he told the ex-president in his letter of May 25, 1891.

The gist of Hayes's reply: Maybe next year.

"You expressed the hope, if I remember rightly, that this year . . ." Du Bois wrote to Hayes in early April 1892, with an update. He had received his master's degree (June 1891) and had also presented his thesis at the annual meeting of the prestigious all-white American Historical Association in Washington, D.C. (December 1891).

The dissertation Du Bois had to write for his Ph.D. would be an expansion of his master's thesis, to be titled "The Suppression of the African Slave Trade to the United States of America, 1638–1870." In this much longer research paper, he would chronicle the growth of slavery and why the importation of kidnapped Africans did not end—was not suppressed—on January 1, 1808, as mandated by law. (Short answer: Greed.)

Du Bois didn't give Hayes the details on his dissertation, but he forcefully asked the Slater Fund to: (1) give him a scholarship; (2) give him a loan; or (3) suggest someone who might lend him the money.

Persistence paid off. The Slater Fund granted Du Bois seven hundred and fifty dollars, half cash, half loan, "to support him one year in Germany at some university," Hayes noted in his journal.

"Some university" was the University of Berlin (as Friedrich-Wilhelms-Universität was known). Du Bois now wanted to earn his Ph.D. from this school. It topped Harvard in the international pecking order.

In mid-July 1892, Du Bois was aboard a Dutch steamer, reaching Rotterdam on the first of August. From there, he went on to Germany, with shore time in Düsseldorf, Cologne, and Frankfurt, then a long stay in Eisenach for German-language immersion and relaxation.

Those weeks in Eisenach, in the shadow of Wartburg Castle, were so entrancing, with wondrous walks in the woods; dancing! dancing! dancing! at the annual ball; and serenading blue-eyed Dora, a daughter of the man in whose boardinghouse he lived.

His encounters with white Europeans were all positive all the time. None had recoiled from or menaced him because of the color of his skin. None would, as he traveled to Berlin, where he arrived in October 1892 and found lodgings at 130A Oranienstrasse.

Economics with Professor Gustav von Schmoller.

Politics with Professor Heinrich von Treitschke.

More economics with Professor Adolf Wagner.

These are some of the courses that would give Du Bois's mental muscle a workout. So did budgeting.

Early on, he reviewed his expenses, from twenty-one-cent lunches ("including beer and tip") to an occasional concert—four hundred bucks a year. "If more economically minded, I might make this $300," he noted in his journal.

Du Bois wanted to penny-pinch so he could travel. And travel he did during breaks, sometimes with a friend—his best was a white Brit, John Dollar—and sometimes solo, seeing a lot of Germany: Munich and Mannheim, Naustadt and Nuremberg, Strassburg and Stuttgart, and climbing the Brocken.

This was chapter three in his "Age of Miracles."

The scrapbook of his mind bulged with memorable countryside and city-street scenes in Germany and other places, including Austria-Hungary (made up of today's Austria and Hungary, and parts of Poland and other nations).

Du Bois fell in love with Europe's cultural offerings, from museums to monuments. As he saw it, white Europeans were better—more human—than their American cousins. Ironic, considering that European nations, with their colonies in Asia, the West Indies, and elsewhere, ruled hundreds of millions of people of color. Great Britain, France, and Germany were among the king culprits in the "Scramble for Africa," which began in the 1870s.

By the early 1900s, and largely through warfare, Europeans would control about ninety percent of Africa, getting rich from the continent's diamonds, gold, and other natural resources and exploiting its people. Great Britain, for example, would rule over Egypt, Nigeria, and present-day Ghana, South Africa, Zambia, and Zimbabwe, among other places. Germany's colonies would include present-day Namibia and Tanzania.

Europeans worked out how they wanted to carve

up Africa during the 1884–1885 Berlin Conference organized by Otto von Bismarck. Du Bois wasn't disturbed by the Scramble for Africa. "I did not question the interpretation which pictured this as the advance of civilization and the benevolent tutelage of barbarians," he later admitted.

Back in Berlin, when Du Bois wasn't at a lecture or in the library, he was often on "a wander" about the city or sketching out tales that swam in his head.

His story "A Fellow of Harvard" was about a "smart but a bit odd" Harvard man named George, who studies in Europe, where he becomes a socialist. Du Bois's occasional drop bys on Socialist Party meetings in Berlin probably inspired this development in the life of George, who has trouble finishing his dissertation. Back in the U.S., George teaches at a school in the South "where his eccentricities get him in trouble with the blacks and his radicalism with the whites." All is not lost. George completes his dissertation. What's more, it is a smashing success!

Haunting all Du Bois's real and imaginative wanders was the anguish of not being able to love his native land. He envied Germans he heard belting out "Das Lied der Deutschen" ("The Song of the Germans"), with its line "Deutschland, Deutschland, über Alles, über Alles in der Welt" ("Germany, Germany above everything, above everything in the world").

Du Bois figured he'd never feel such pounding patriotism. That depressed him. It also spurred him even more to be a man of mark, as he promised himself on his twenty-fifth birthday.

The day before, he treated himself to a concert, Schubert's *Unfinished Symphony*. Later that wintry night, he held "a curious little ceremony" in his room. There was wine, oil, and candles. There was a "Sacrifice to the Zeitgeist" (German for Spirit of the Time). He then dedicated his library to his mother.

High points from the next day, his birthday—February 23, 1893—included a marvelous midday meal with a friend named Einderhof. It was one of the best days of his life Du Bois wrote in his journal that night, rejoicing "as a strong man to run a race."

Was that arrogance? he wondered. Self-confidence? Or was it "the silent call of the world spirit that makes me feel that I am royal and that beneath my sceptre a world of kings shall bow." As he felt the "hot dark blood of that forefather" (presumably Tom) "born king of men" beating at his heart—

"And I know that I am either a genius or a fool."

Or drunk?

"O I wonder what I am—I wonder what the world is—I wonder if Life is worth the striving."

Du Bois pondered Life's dimensions: the Good (its end), the Beautiful (its soul), and the True (its being). "Mayhap God is the fourth, but for that very reason incomprehensible."

Whether Du Bois had ever been a Christian (versus a church-goer) is unknowable. By now, he was not; however, he believed in Jesus' teachings about how people should treat each other. For the rest of his life, he would often speak and write in religious terms, ever aware, ever feeling the power of certain words. Like "the Devil." Like "Heaven." Like "God."

Years into the future, a Cuban priest would write Du Bois, asking if he believed in God.

"If by being 'a believer in God' you mean a belief in a person of vast power who consciously rules the universe for the good of mankind, I answer No," Du

Bois would reply. "If on the other hand you mean by 'God' a vague Force which, in some incomprehensible way, dominates all life and change, then I answer, Yes; I recognize such Force, and if you wish to call it God, I do not object."

Back in 1893, on his twenty-fifth birthday, Du Bois was communing with the Force it seems, as he committed himself to the Good, the Beautiful, the True, in his "striving to make my life all that life may be."

Thus he vowed to "work for the rise of the Negro people, taking for granted that their best development means the best development of the world."

Thus he declared: "These are my plans: to make a name in science, to make a name in literature and thus to raise my race. Or perhaps to raise a visible empire in Africa thro' England, France or Germany." He was still a booster of European imperialism.

One thing Du Bois would not get through Germany was a Ph.D. The Slater Fund honored his first request for a renewal of financial aid but not the second. A Harvard Ph.D. would have to do.

He was homeward bound late spring 1894, experiencing as much of Europe as he could. Paris was where he spent most of May. June found him in London, enjoying a farewell few days with his friend John Dollar before boarding a U.S.-bound ship out of Southampton.

The tradeoff for stretching out his stay was traveling steerage, enduring many beastly hours during the nine-day voyage below deck with about three hundred other souls. Austrians and Americans (black and white). Greeks and Germans. Jews and Gentiles. Some were seemingly noble, others rapscallions and rogues. Some poor of mind; others, like him, only poor of pocket. The non-blacks were likely to have a better shot at the American Dream than his kith and kin if they—the Antonios, Dimitris, Johanns—did what millions of Europeans did over the years: became un-foreign, became "white."

In mid-June 1894, W. E. B. Du Bois returned to "'nigger'-hating America!"

His Age of Miracles was over.

FOUR

"PRESIDENT WASHINGTON SIR!"

July 27, 1894, posted from Great Barrington.

President Washington was Booker T. Washington, head of Tuskegee Normal and Industrial Institute (now Tuskegee University) in Tuskegee, Alabama.

Du Bois was applying for a job, preferably as a teacher of history and social science, but he told Washington that he was flexible. "Your wife knows of me," he added. Washington, twice widowed, was then married to Fisk grad Margaret Murray.

Du Bois applied to other majority-black schools. They included Hampton Institute, Howard University (D.C.), and the first one to send him a positive reply: the African Methodist Episcopal Church's

Wilberforce University, in Xenia, Ohio. Wilberforce offered Du Bois eight hundred dollars a year to teach Greek and Latin. Straightaway, he accepted.

Within days came other offers. "Can give mathematics here if terms suit," began Booker T. Washington's telegram. Du Bois kept his word to Wilberforce, though, and was soon off to Ohio, excited, expectant.

Wilberforce was the pits for Du Bois. On top of Latin and Greek, he had to teach German, English, and history. A heavy workload was no problem, but he only *liked* it when it was on his terms. He would have happily taught a hundred courses if sociology were one of them. No sociology, he was told.

What's more, the university was cash poor. Instead of a first-class library, it had but "a few piles of old books."

Wilberforce's religiosity was another rub. Du Bois knew beforehand that it was an AME school, but not that revivals, prayer meetings, and other religious activities were so pervasive and virtually mandatory. Du Bois wouldn't fake faith to fit in. He made

Dapper Du Bois, shown here in 1900, began sporting a goatee in Germany.

that clear early on when he happened upon a student prayer meeting.

"Professor Du Bois will lead us in prayer," a well-meaning student called out.

"No, he won't."

Like his character George, Du Bois was definitely considered "a bit odd."

While Du Bois had a dim view of organized religion, he revered many clerics. One was Wilberforce's guest speaker for commencement day June 1895: Episcopal priest Alexander Crummell.

Coal black, brilliant, and regal in bearing, seventy-six-year-old Alexander Crummell, a native New Yorker, was a graduate of a British school, Cambridge University's Queens College. This son of an African once enslaved had spent about twenty years as a missionary in Africa. Crummell's mission field was Liberia, the West African nation settled in the 1820s by blacks from America.

After Crummell was back in the U.S. for good in the early 1870s, he started St. Luke's Episcopal Church in D.C. Years earlier, he had been pastor of a different

St. Luke's, in New Haven. Its treasurer was another Alexander: Alexander Du Bois.

W. E. B. knew this. When his grandfather died back in 1887, W. E. B. had inherited a few hundred dollars and something more valuable: the old man's leather-bound journals. Through them, grandson began to learn of grandfather's life, including his dabblings in poetry. W. E. B. later wrote of having private time with Crummell when he was at Wilberforce, but left no record of their conversation.

Crummell's commencement address is no mystery. It was "The Solution of Problems: The Duty and Destiny of Man." In it, he stressed that people did not live by bread alone and that behind all strivings for life's necessities—food, shelter, clothing—was an even more profound problem.

Labor strikes, for example, weren't just about getting higher wages or better working conditions, but rather about "some absorbing moral problem which agitated the souls of men." Crummell insisted that it was the duty of people like Du Bois and the Wilberforce grads to devote themselves to alleviating what agitated the souls of black folks. Black America's best and brightest were the only <u>hope</u> for the black masses, he believed.

A few months after Crummell addressed Wilberforce grads, Booker T. Washington spoke at the opening day of the Cotton States and International Exposition in Atlanta, Georgia.

On September 18, 1895, before a largely white crowd, Washington offered his solution to the "Negro Problem," at least as it pertained to the South. His main idea: "In all things that are purely social [blacks and whites] can be as separate as the five fingers, yet one as the hand in all things essential to mutual progress."

Things purely social included parks, restaurants, train cars, and schools. Mutual progress was industry and a strong economy.

The upshot of the speech was a call for compromise.

White people: Let blacks (especially those like the graduates of his vocational school) have economic opportunities—for example, the freedom to run their farms, blacksmith shops, brick-making factories, and other enterprises without harassment from KKK types.

Black people: Work hard, save your money, be law-abiding citizens, and trust that in time whites will deem you worthy of civil rights. "Agitation" for "social equality is the extremest folly," said Washington.

"The speech stamps Booker T. Washington as a wise and a safe leader" for blacks, proclaimed the *Atlanta Constitution*, a white-owned newspaper.

Washington was stone-cold practical and operating on the stoop-to-conquer principle. This son of the South knew that if he called for radical change, Tuskegee Institute might be burned to the ground. He was a bulldog when it came to his school, and tenacious since his youth.

Washington was Virginia-born and slavery-born, the product of a white man's rape of his enslaved mother. After freedom came, young Booker made the most of a makeshift school in West Virginia, while working as a manual laborer. When he heard about Hampton Institute, he walked there (about five hundred miles), then worked his way through school, graduating with honors (1875). He was the number-one protégé of Hampton's white founder, General Samuel Chapman Armstrong, who had commanded black troops during the Civil War.

Armstrong believed that vocational education, not a liberal arts education, was the key to blacks rising. When the American Missionary Association decided to start a school like Hampton in Tuskegee, Alabama, Armstrong recommended Washington as the man to head it. In 1881, when Du Bois was in high school and probably still ga-ga over Macaulay's *The History of England*, twenty-five-year-old Washington was transforming a few shacks into a school. For this cause, he cultivated the public persona of a Negro deferential—some would say groveling—to whites. That's how he gained many white "friends" and white dollars to build up his school. More money and support from white philanthropists flowed Tuskegee's way after Washington's Atlanta speech.

Du Bois sent Washington a telegram of congratulations, calling that speech "a word fitly spoken." Freedom to earn a living and build up economically, he reasoned, was nothing to sneeze at. In early January 1896, Du Bois wrote Washington again, asking on the sly for a job: "If you hear of any opening which you think I am fitted to fill kindly let me know."

By then, Du Bois's dissertation, "Suppression," had

been approved and the twenty-eight-year-old scholar had made history: the first black to earn a Ph.D. from Harvard University. What's more, as he told Washington, "Suppression" was to be the first book in a new and prestigious series: Harvard Historical Studies.

A smashing success!

Still, no new job offers. Not from Tuskegee or any other school. One of the finest and best-credentialed American minds soldiered on at Wilberforce.

One of Du Bois's delights there was student Nina Gomer, a shy beauty who became his wife. Nina and "Will," as she would always call her beloved, married on May 12, 1896. It was a small affair in the home of her father (a hotel chef) in Cedar Rapids, Iowa. (Other than a minister, only Nina's father, stepmother, and little sister were on hand.) Shortly after the wedding, the newlyweds returned to Wilberforce. They started their married life in a two-room apartment in Shorter Hall, the men's dorm in which Professor Du Bois had been living.

A few days later came a damning day for Du Bois, his wife, and all blacks in the U.S. for generations to come. On May 18, 1896, the U.S. Supreme Court delivered its decision in the case *Plessy v. Ferguson*, sanctioning segregation of public facilities. Many blacks would have had no problem with segregation had separate facilities been equal, but this would not be the case as city after city, state after state in the South, went Jim Crow—that is, made segregation the law, dooming blacks to substandard facilities like bad schools and denying them access to simple pleasures like parks.

Meanwhile, Du Bois was on fire to find another job. The saying "chance favors the prepared mind" proved true for him yet again.

"Are ready to appoint you for one year at nine hundred dollars maximum," read a June 8, 1896, telegram from an official at the University of Pennsylvania in Philadelphia. The appointment wasn't for a teaching post but for a research job: to study the city's blacks, focusing on the Seventh Ward. This was a poor neighborhood in which about twenty percent of Philly's forty thousand blacks lived. The people behind the study wanted to prove, Du Bois recalled, that Philly was "going to the dogs" because of blacks, whom many thought were inherently hopeless.

Du Bois had his own agenda: "The Negro problem was in my mind a matter of systematic investigation and intelligent understanding. The world was thinking wrong about race, because it did not know. The ultimate evil was stupidity. The cure for it was knowledge based on scientific investigation." Race was not destiny, but circumstances and lack of opportunity almost always were.

Du Bois's confidence in his brain power got a boost shortly before he and Nina moved to Philly. In the summer of 1896, *Suppression* was published. His study of the slave trade ended with an appeal to the world: do not allow "through carelessness and moral cowardice, any social evil to grow." Had the nation's founders been true to the Declaration of Independence and abolished slavery, they would have spared the nation a shameful history and there would have been no Civil War. "From this we may conclude that it behooves nations as well as men to do things at the very moment when they ought to be done," declared Du Bois.

The American Historical Association's journal

called *Suppression* "a valuable review of an important subject."

His Philadelphia study would be important, too.

For more than a year, Du Bois would gather data on black Philly's institutions, businesses, and people—going door to door, questionnaires in hand, conducting some five thousand interviews in the Seventh Ward and some spot investigations of other wards, including the Thirteenth, where many of Philly's better-off blacks lived. The data Du Bois collected—education, employment, marital status, family size, health, finances—became tables, charts, and graphs.

Crime, alcoholism, and higher rates of death and disease were among the problems plaguing blacks in the Seventh Ward. Du Bois's findings and conclusions became the landmark work of urban sociology *The Philadelphia Negro: A Social Study* (published in 1899).

The book's chapter on "Pauperism and Alcoholism" has in its list of "typical families" the following:

No. 2—South Tenth Street. Five in the family; widow and children out of work, and had sold the bed to pay for expense of a sick child.

No. 9—Lombard Street. Five in family; wife white; living in one room; hard cases; rum and lies; pretended one child was dead in order to get aid.

Du Bois looked down on many of the people he studied, seeing them as their own worst enemies and writing them off as trifling. He also found blacks barely making it or in crisis because of circumstances beyond their control. The color line was a killer.

There was a brushmaker who couldn't get a white firm even to look at samples of his handiwork. A baker had a hoped-for door of opportunity slammed in his face with "We don't work no niggers here."

Upholstery, printing, carpentry, bricklaying—a host of blacks were blocked from doing work for which they were qualified because of racism. No wonder 80 percent of Philly's black men age twenty-one and older worked as unskilled laborers and as servants—the lowest paying jobs.

Blacks also faced pay inequity—in effect being robbed. Examples included a black cementer earning $1.75 a day when a white cementer made $2 or $3 a day.

Du Bois often organized and analyzed data in the single room that was his and Nina's home. It was in the Seventh Ward above a restaurant and on a block "where kids played intriguing games like 'cops and lady bums'; and where in the night when pistols popped, you didn't get up lest you find you couldn't."

Amid all this, the Du Boises enjoyed wedded bliss, with many precious moments around Christmas 1896. When Nina asked how much they could spend on the holidays—"I sat down and figured carefully: for there was the sewing machine to pay for out of this month's salary, and [a] doctor's bill, and one other debt—an old family friend." Bottom line: five bucks apiece. Fifteen cents was spent on a Christmas tree. Christmas morning Will got neckties and suspenders; Nina, an umbrella.

In early February 1897, the couple had something else to celebrate. Nina was pregnant.

Du Bois didn't want his wife to spend her pregnancy in a slum—didn't want their baby born on a block where kids played cops and lady bums. He sent Nina to stay with family members in the Berkshires until she had their baby. Her Will remained Philly-based. His big study wasn't the only thing on his plate.

Early March, 1897: He was in D.C. for the first meeting of the American Negro Academy. Months earlier, he had been in D.C. for a meeting with a handful of other men. They were there at Alexander Crummell's urging to form an association of intellectuals who would meet and exchange ideas and publish random papers of thought and discoveries.

Members of the American Negro Academy (ANA) included the austere Presbyterian minister Francis Grimké, a graduate of Princeton Theological Seminary. Another was the brilliant Kelly Miller, a Howard University mathematics and sociology professor who had earned his bachelor's at Howard and did some graduate work at Johns Hopkins.

Du Bois's contribution to the first ANA meeting was the paper "The Conservation of Races." In it, he maintained that all peoples possessed particular gifts and therefore all peoples needed to be preserved— blacks included, and especially so, as they had not yet given their gift to the world.

While in D.C. for the ANA meeting, Du Bois met with the head of the U.S. Bureau of Labor Statistics. He wanted Du Bois to conduct studies on black America.

Mid-March–June: Du Bois continued researching black Philly and decided on the focus of his labor bureau project: the black community of Farmville, Virginia.

July–August: He lived in Farmville gathering data for the making of the 1898 labor bureau bulletin *The Negroes of Farmville, Virginia: A Social Study*. As if that wasn't enough to keep him busy, while in Virginia, Du Bois attended a conference on black life held in Norfolk and sponsored by Hampton Institute.

Along the way, a major magazine, the *Atlantic Monthly*, asked Du Bois for an article on the hopes of black folks. When it appeared, readers discovered that W. E. B. Du Bois, Ph.D., had the soul of a poet along with a scholar's brain.

FIVE

"BETWEEN ME AND the other world there is ever an unasked question," began Du Bois's essay "Strivings of the Negro People," in the August 1897 *Atlantic Monthly.*

The other world was the white world. The unasked question: "How does it feel to be a problem?"

It hurt.

Du Bois recalled that in his youth, despite the cheers of whites like Frank Hosmer, he had always felt "shut out" from the other world by "a vast veil."

And being black, said Du Bois, meant dealing with a "double-consciousness."

> It is a peculiar sensation, this double-consciousness, this sense of always looking

at one's self through the eyes of others, of measuring one's soul by the tape of a world that looks on in amused contempt and pity. One ever feels his two-ness,—an American, a Negro; two souls, two thoughts, two un-reconciled strivings; two warring ideals in one dark body, whose dogged strength alone keeps it from being torn asunder.

Black Americans longed for "oneness"—a merging of the two selves—not wanting to "Africanize America, for America has too much to teach the world and Africa," and not wanting to "to bleach [their] Negro blood in a flood of white Americanism," because they believed that "Negro blood has yet a message for the world." The ultimate hope of black folks was to live in a nation where it was possible to be "a Negro and an American without being cursed and spit upon" and "without losing the opportunity of self-development."

Many people have accepted Du Bois's assessment of the souls of black Americans as a blanket truth, as opposed to being true of people like Du Bois who wanted, along with equality of opportunity, for whites to accept them as "American." In contrast, there are and always have been blacks who recognized that "American" was typically associated with whiteness, but who simply rejected that notion and considered themselves black and American, needing no affirmation from whites, suffering no two-ness, never living split-souled lives nor feeling on the verge of being torn asunder.

And many blacks did want to bleach their "Negro blood," so to speak. The rap on sub-Saharan Africa, the ancestral home of most American blacks, was that it was a land of savages whose features, including dark skin and kinky hair, were ugly. This led many blacks to cosmetic extremes, such as trying to lighten their skin with chemicals. It also led to some light-skinned blacks taking great pride in their color and dark-skinned blacks feeling ashamed—some, not all. Alexander Crummell was proud that he had no so-called "white blood."

The rest of "Strivings" recalled black strides during Reconstruction and the agony of the rollback of rights. Still, said Du Bois, blacks clung to "the dogged hope" for a just nation. So did Du Bois, especially after he became a father.

Nina had a boy—Burghardt Gomer Du Bois—on October 2, 1897. Du Bois desperately wanted his son to grow up in a more enlightened world. He also wanted him to have a better place to live in the short run. When Nina and the baby joined him in Philly they didn't live in that Seventh Ward room, but in a nicer place, and temporarily. After he wrapped up his Philadelphia study, the family moved to the city of a hundred hills.

"The hundred hills of Atlanta are not all crowned with factories," Du Bois later wrote in recalling Georgia's capital. "On one [hill], toward the west, the setting sun throws three buildings in bold relief against the sky."

This was Atlanta University (AU, today Clark Atlanta University). One of the buildings was South Hall, the men's dormitory where the Du Boises had an apartment.

Back in 1896, during a trip to Philly, AU president Horace Bumstead, a white New Englander, had recruited Du Bois. Like Fisk, AU was founded after the Civil War by whites who didn't think a liberal arts education for blacks the extremest folly.

Neither was sociology.

As AU's new professor of history and economics, Du Bois could teach sociology to his heart's content. Bumstead also made him chief of the school's fledgling annual conferences on black life. With Du Bois in charge, each conference would focus on a specific aspect of black America to get the big picture of its good, bad, and ugly. Conference reports, he hoped, would guide reform efforts where needed and give encouragement where deserved.

Unlike Wilberforce, AU was not the pits for Du Bois—but for some students he was Du Bois the Dreaded. Other students appreciated his toughness. One remembered with fondness the way "he pulled on your intellectual powers with broad reading and open discussion."

Du Bois soon had students doing research papers on topics that were pure Du Bois, such as "The Negro Merchant in Atlanta." In spring 1899, he had Negro lynch victims on his mind.

In April, in Newnan, Georgia, about forty miles southwest of Atlanta, a black man identified as Sam Hose was being hunted for killing his white employer,

Alfred Cranford, in a pay-related dispute. According to the *Atlanta Constitution*, Mrs. Cranford claimed that after the black man murdered her husband, he committed other outrages, including raping her. The *Atlanta Constitution* offered a $500 reward for Hose.

When Du Bois heard about the hunt for this man, he whipped up a letter calling for attention to facts and a fair trial, a letter he hoped the *Atlanta Constitution* would publish. He was en route to the newspaper when—

"I did not get there. On the way news met me: Sam Hose had been lynched, and they said that his knuckles were on exhibition at a grocery store farther down on Mitchell Street, along which I was walking."

A mob had decided that Hose didn't deserve a trial, but rather castration and burning. After the corpse cooled, people got out their knives and scrambled for souvenirs.

About seven hundred blacks were lynched in the 1890s. Few of them had committed a crime—not that lynching would have been just if they had. In most cases of white-on-black vigilante violence, white law officials had no interest in bringing the criminals to

With wife and son.

justice. So it was with the lynching of Sam Hose, whose real name, as it turns out, was Tom Wilkes, and who had indeed killed his employer, but claims of other crimes were apparently the product of the rumor mill.

A month after the lynching, the Du Boises were consumed by a greater, more personal grief. On May 24, 1899, their two-year-old son died.

What his parents thought was a bad cold was diphtheria, a bacteria-born disease. As little Burghardt lay dying, his father raced around the city of a hundred hills looking for medical help. He couldn't find one of the few black doctors. (Rare was the white doctor who would have a black patient.)

For Nina and Will, the idea of burying their son in the mean and bloody South was unthinkable.

"We seemed to rumble down an unknown street behind a little white bundle of posies, with the shadow of a song in our ears." The couple was walking to the train station, for a journey to Great Barrington to bury Burghardt. Before them, a horse-drawn cart bore the little coffin. White passersby "did not say much,—they only glanced and said, 'Niggers!'"

There is no getting over the loss of a child. There is only coping or hoping to cope. Nina fell into a depression. Her resolute Will worked. After burying Burghardt, and with Nina still up north, he was back in Atlanta. As scheduled, he presided over the May 30–31 AU conference. (That year it was on black-owned businesses. The findings included that the number was pretty paltry.)

In 1900, Du Bois's work included a trip to Europe.

Between April and November 1900, some 60

million people would visit the City of Light for the Paris Exposition, a salute to nineteenth-century achievements and a *Hello!* to new-century innovations. (A moving sidewalk would be among the marvels on display.)

The U.S. Congress allocated over $1 million for the American pavilion at this Paris world's fair, with no plans to include anything about black achievement. Fisk grad Tom Calloway, a clerk in the War Department, contacted prominent blacks about changing that. It wasn't about vanity but about countering negative stereotypes spread around the world.

In response to Calloway's campaign, Booker T. Washington appealed to President McKinley. Also on the case was North Carolina Representative George Henry White, the only black in Congress. (There had been more than twenty earlier, during Reconstruction.) White pushed for twenty-five thousand in funding. Congress granted fifteen thousand for a "Negro Exhibit," with Tom Calloway its chief. Calloway turned to several people to curate segments of the exhibit.

Back in college, Calloway had been the *Fisk Herald's*

business manager when Du Bois was its editor in chief. Now he asked Du Bois for a display on black Georgia, the state with the largest black population (about 1 million out of 2.2 million).

There was no way that Du Bois wasn't going to take his handiwork to Paris and supervise its setup. When he sailed in mid-June, Nina, now five months pregnant, stayed behind. As she had before, she spent most of her pregnancy up north with the Burghardts.

The stats in Du Bois's exhibit included the rise in the number of blacks attending public school between 1870 and 1897 (from 10,000 to 180,000). Du Bois did more than give factoids of black progress. He *showed* it with photographs.

The dignity on display included stately homes with chandeliers, pianos, and other touches of class by Victorian standards. The people were impressive, too:

Well-groomed men in suits and ties and high, stiff collars.

Carefully coifed women in ruffle-collared Sunday best and leg-o'-mutton-sleeved walking dresses.

Perky children, neat and clean.

Hard workers, from laborers to laundresses, looking industrious and striving.

The Negro Exhibit won a Grand Prize, and various facets received medals. For his part, Du Bois was awarded a gold medal.

After Paris came London.

Du Bois was among the roughly thirty blacks answering a call issued the previous year by Henry Sylvester Williams, a Trinidad-born attorney. Williams was the force behind London's African Association, a group of West Indian professionals devoted to black solidarity. Alexander Crummell, who had died in 1898, would have been proud of the three-day conference in London's Westminster Town Hall (July 23–25, 1900).

Photographer John Archer and musician-composer Samuel Coleridge-Taylor, both Londoners, were among the participants. Also there, the Haitian Benito Sylvain, aide-de-camp to Emperor Menelik II of Ethiopia. (His army had trounced Italian troops a few years back, and thus saved Ethiopia from becoming an Italian colony.)

In addition to Du Bois, the American delegates

included Oberlin College grad and the ANA's only female member, Anna Julia Cooper. Du Bois adored her collection of essays, *A Voice from the South* (1892)—a pioneering black feminist text—along with the work that Cooper did: teaching at one of nation's finest public schools, D.C.'s Washington Colored School, better known as the M Street School.

Du Bois, Cooper, and the other conferees created the Pan-African Association (Pan is Greek for "all"). Du Bois drafted the association's manifesto, "To the Nations of the World."

"The problem of the twentieth century," Du Bois declared early on in this address, "is the problem of the colour line, the question as to how far differences of race, which show themselves chiefly in the colour of the skin and the texture of the hair, are going to be made, hereafter, the basis of denying to over half the world the right of sharing to their utmost ability the opportunities and privileges of modern civilization."

With advances in communications (telegram and telegraph) and transportation (faster ships and trains) the world was getting smaller. People of color were "bound to have a great influence upon the world in the future, by reason of sheer numbers and physical contact," Du Bois pointed out. If these people were given decent education and a shot at developing their skills and abilities, they would be assets to their societies—and thus "have a beneficial effect upon the world and hasten progress."

This was not a call for an end to colonialism but for a more humane colonialism. The thinking was that the colonized wouldn't be worthy of self-rule until they had abandoned many of their traditions and were westernized.

Just as famous as his two-ness theory is Du Bois's assertion that the problem of the new century would be "the problem of the colour line." The idea that racism would be a problem—pretty obvious. But *the* problem? Even Du Bois would one day disagree with himself.

A few months after Du Bois returned to the U.S., Nina had a girl, on October 21, 1900. The baby was a Sunday's child like her father. They named her Nina Yolande, but would call her Yolande.

As the family resumed its life together in Atlanta, thirty-one-year-old Du Bois continued to press for a better world by lecturing, studying, teaching, organizing AU conferences and editing their reports.

And by continuing to write. Hardly a month went by that he was not in print, serving up insights on black life past and present, and sometimes book reviews.

The July 1901 *Dial* magazine carried his say on Booker T. Washington's autobiography *Up from Slavery*, a brisk seller.

What Du Bois wrote was less a review and more a notice that not all blacks worshipped at the altar of Booker T. Washington and his "gospel of Work and Money." Francis Grimké and Kelly Miller were among those who thought that Washington's way was weak, Du Bois reported. "They believe, therefore, also in the higher education of Fisk and Atlanta Universities."

So did he, of course. "They" meant "we."

"They believe in self-assertion and ambition; and they believe in the right of suffrage for blacks on the same terms with whites."

By then, more blacks in the South had been disfranchised. Louisiana, for example, had a poll tax, a literacy test, *and* a "grandfather clause." Anyone who had a forebear able to vote on January 1, 1867—three years *before* black men got the vote—was exempt from the tax and the test.

Du Bois's articles kept coming in 1902. Standouts include "Of the Training of Black Men," in the September *Atlantic Monthly*. This essay was a testament to the value of college-educated blacks to the black community and thus to the nation.

There was and always would be a percentage of young blacks wanting and well suited for a college education, Du Bois argued in advancing the Crummell doctrine. By virtue of their education, they would be the natural, necessary leaders of their people, lifting as they climbed. The "Talented Tenth," Du Bois called them. (This wasn't a literal 10 percent of the black population, but his metaphor for that corps of blacks who were highly educated, very accomplished, or both. Also, in most cases, Du Bois's "men" was shorthand for "men and women.")

As more people encountered the mind and passions of W. E. B. Du Bois in periodicals, requests for speaking engagements rose.

Monroe Trotter contacted Du Bois in the fall of

1902, beseeching him to come to Boston to address a black literary society. Trotter had changed since their days at Harvard (where he became its first black Phi Beta Kappa and earned both a bachelor's and a master's degree). With the rising tide of racism, Trotter now believed that it was a very good thing for blacks to herd together, wherever, whenever, forever. In 1901, with George Forbes, a graduate of the Bay State's Amherst College, Trotter launched a newspaper, *The Guardian*. Its motto: "For every right, with all thy might."

Trotter wanted Du Bois to speak in Boston in January 1903. This was the year that the peripatetic professor became something of a star.

SIX

"HEREIN LIE BURIED many things which if read with patience may show the strange meaning of being black here at the dawning of the Twentieth Century."

February 1, 1903, the day Du Bois finished "The Forethought," as he called the introduction to his book *The Souls of Black Folk,* published in April 1903.

In "The Forethought" Du Bois again declared the color line to be the problem of the twentieth century. In the rest of the book, he offered a rich mix of memoir, fiction, history, and sociology. Most chapters open with verse by a white American or European writer followed by a bar or two from a spiritual.

Many of the essays in *Souls* are revised versions of previously published gems. They include "Strivings of the Negro People" (now "Of Our Spiritual Strivings") and "Of the Training of Black Men" (which kept its title).

One of the book's five original pieces is "Of the Coming of John," a short story about the positive transformation at a Northern school of a Southern young man, whose life ends in tragedy after he returns home.

Before that story comes a tribute to Alexander Crummell. "Instinctively I bowed before this man, as one bows before the prophets of the world," wrote Du Bois of their first meeting at Wilberforce. He remembered his idol as one who "never faltered, he seldom complained; he simply worked, inspiring the young, rebuking the old, helping the weak, guiding the strong."

The most personal piece, also new, has the title of a spiritual: "Of the Passing of the First-Born."

In it, Du Bois relived his son's birth: "the fear of fatherhood mingled wildly with the joy of creation."

Then came Burghardt's sickness, his trembling hands, his fevered face, his "wasting, wasting away."

Finally: "He died at eventide, when the sun lay like a brooding sorrow above the western hills, veiling its face; when the winds spoke not, and the trees, the great green trees he loved, stood motionless."

Du Bois dedicated *Souls* to his children:

To
Burghardt and Yolande
THE LOST AND THE FOUND

Souls's most explosive essay was "Of Mr. Booker T. Washington and Others."

By then, Washington was well under way in building the "Tuskegee Machine," a network of black institutions and individuals promoting his views and stifling dissent—some because they were true believers, others because it meant a payday for them. Washington had a lot of power. A white politician considering a token black for a city, state, or federal job might ask—Who does Booker find worthy? A white philanthropist inclined to make a donation to a black school—What does Booker think?

The Wizard, he was called.

And what had blacks gotten during the Wizard's ascendancy, eight years after his "Atlanta Compromise" speech? Du Bois asked, then answered in "Of Mr. Booker T. Washington and Others":

1. The disfranchisement of the Negro.
2. The legal creation of a distinct status of

civil inferiority for the Negro.

3. The steady withdrawal of aid from institutions for the higher training of the Negro.

By 1902, Virginia, Texas, Tennessee, the Carolinas, Georgia, Florida, and Arkansas, had, like Mississippi and Louisiana, adopted laws that blighted the black vote. So had Washington's Alabama. In 1898, it had about 180,000 registered black voters. In 1902, roughly 3,000.

Though Washington had secretly funded a case challenging black disenfranchisement, he persisted in denouncing open protest of racial injustices. Though he had sent his daughter to a predominantly white liberal arts college (Wellesley), he publicly ridiculed blacks studying the likes of Plato over proper plowing.

Washington was complicit in the degradation of blacks, Du Bois believed. So long as the Wizard—and the nation—defended the racial status quo "we must unceasingly and firmly oppose them," he insisted.

Souls's last essay, "The Sorrow Songs," is a primer and paean to the spirituals: music telling "of death and suffering and unvoiced longing toward a truer world, of misty wanderings and hidden ways."

" I walk through the church yard
   " To lay this body down
" I know moon-rise, I know star-rise;
" I walk in the moonlight, I walk in the star-light;
" I'll lie in the grave and stretch out my arms,
" I'll go to judgment in the evening of the day
" And my soul and thy soul shall meet that day
      " When I lay this body down."
                    Negro Song.

They that walked in darkness sang
songs in the olden days — Sorrow Songs —
for they were weary at heart. And so before
each that I have written I have set
a phrase, a haunting echo of these weird
old songs in which the soul of the black
slave spoke to men. Ever since I was
a child these songs have stirred me
strangely. They came to me out of the
South unknown to me, one by one, and
yet at once I knew them as of me and of
mine. Then in after years when I came
to Nashville I saw the great temple builded
of these songs towering over the pale city. To me

Du Bois opened "The Sorrow Songs" with lyrics from "Lay This Body Down," followed by musical notation from "Wrestling Jacob." Other music and lyrics within the text include his ancestor's "Do bana coba, gene me, gene me!" The finale was a lengthy notation from "Let Us Cheer the Weary Traveller."

Let us cheer the weary traveller,
Cheer the weary traveller.
Let us cheer the weary traveller
Along the heavenly way.

"'THE SOULS OF BLACK FOLK' SHOULD BE READ AND STUDIED BY EVERY PERSON, WHITE AND BLACK," declared the black-owned *Ohio Enterprise* out of Cincinnati.

The Nation, a white-owned magazine out of New York City, praised *Souls* for the way it conveyed "an aching sense of the wrongs done to [the author's] people, heretofore and still."

Trotter's *Guardian* applauded the book's "vigor, spontaneity, and spirituality."

Writing from Chicago in May 1903, another black journalist and also an anti-lynching crusader, Ida B. Wells-Barnett, wrote Du Bois that *Souls* had been the buzz at a recent social event. As she recalled in her autobiography, after reading the piece on Booker T. Washington, she and her husband, attorney Ferdinand Barnett, recognized like never before "that Mr. Washington's views on industrial education had become an obsession with the white people of this country." It was time to show them that no one educational program "could fit the needs of an entire race."

Du Bois also heard from J. Douglas Wetmore, a lawyer in Jacksonville, Florida. Fresh off his second reading of *Souls*, Wetmore just had to thank Du Bois for the book—on behalf of all black people. He also proclaimed Du Bois the only black soul "worthy to be classed" with Frederick Douglass (who had died back in 1895).

"Professor Du Bois I am going to thank you, as though it had been a personal favor, for your book," wrote Jessie Fauset, a member of Philly's black middle class, attending Cornell University in Ithaca, New York. "It hurt you to write that book, didn't it?" this young woman asked.

Though *Souls* boosted Du Bois's visibility, it didn't sell as well as Washington's *Up from Slavery*. *Souls* was largely scorned or ridiculed by white-run Southern periodicals and by black-owned ones that were part of the Tuskegee Machine.

Oddly enough, Washington and Du Bois were still on speaking terms.

Long before *Souls* came out, Du Bois had already been scheduled to lecture at Tuskegee, in the summer of 1903. While there, he dined with the Washingtons at The Oaks, their elegant fourteen-room home.

There is no record of the dinner conversation. Months earlier, Washington had offered Du Bois a better-paying post at Tuskegee—with a house to boot—but Du Bois feared that if he went to Tuskegee he would be muzzled. In the summer of 1903, Washington may still have hoped that he could win Du Bois over to his side, for the author of *Souls* wasn't his most vitriolic critic.

Monroe Trotter called Washington the "Benedict Arnold of the Negro race" (among other things) and regularly lambasted him in the *Guardian*. In August 1903, Trotter was chomping at the bit to confront him in person when the Wizard was in Boston for a speaking engagement at a black church.

Washington was booed and hissed in Boston. A war of words, then scuffling, then fisticuffs broke out between Bookerites and anti-Bookerites. From atop a chair, Trotter shouted out a list of questions—taunts, really.

"Are the rope and the torch all the race is to get under your leadership?"

Charged with being the instigator of what became known as the "Boston Riot," Trotter was sentenced to thirty days in jail.

Perhaps because Du Bois happened to be in Boston shortly after the incident and decried Trotter's arrest, Washington believed that Du Bois had engineered the fracas. The Wizard told his benefactors as much. A smear on Du Bois was a smear on AU, which received funds (though never as much) from some philanthropists who supported Tuskegee, like investment banker George Foster Peabody. He put the screws on AU president Bumstead, who then implored Du Bois to put Peabody's suspicions to rest.

In his letter to Peabody, Du Bois said he had nothing to do with the so-called Boston Riot. He did not, however, denounce Trotter as Peabody probably hoped. Du Bois had thought Trotter's tactics tacky, but he praised his "unselfishness, pureness of heart and indomitable energy" at a time when "every energy is being used to put black men back into slavery"—and Washington was "leading the way backward." Bumstead wished Du Bois had left that part out.

Readers were reminded of Du Bois's strategy for the way forward when *The Negro Problem* appeared in September 1903. This anthology of essays by prominent blacks included "Industrial Education for the Negro" by Booker T. and "The Talented Tenth" by W. E. B.

As Du Bois stood his ground, he called on others to join him. He exhorted blacks to fight for their rights "unceasingly, and if they fail, die trying," in his essay "The Parting of the Ways," which ran in the April 1904 *World Today*.

In October, the *Independent* published a more pulsing piece from his pen: "Credo" (Latin for "I believe").

SEVEN

"I BELIEVE IN God who made of one blood all races that dwell on earth. I believe that all men, black and brown and white, are brothers, varying, through Time and Opportunity, in form and gift and feature, but differing in no essential particular, and alike in soul and in the possibility of infinite development.

"Especially do I believe in the Negro Race; in the beauty of its genius, the sweetness of its soul and its strength in that meekness which shall yet inherit this turbulent earth.

"I believe in pride of race and lineage and self; in pride of self so deep as to scorn injustice to other selves."

Du Bois also believed that the color line was the work of "the Devil and his angels" and that "the wicked conquest of weaker and darker nations by nations whiter and stronger but foreshadows the death of that strength." How he longed for a heaven on earth.

> I believe in Liberty for all men; the space to stretch their arms and their souls; the right to breathe and the right to vote, the freedom to choose their friends, enjoy the sunshine and ride on the railroads, uncursed by color; thinking, dreaming, working as they will in a kingdom of God and love.

Other newspapers soon reprinted Du Bois's roughly five-hundred-word prose poem, "Credo." It was reproduced on card stock suitable for framing and on scrolls suitable for recitation. What Martin Luther King Jr.'s "I Have a Dream" would be to future generations, "Credo" was to black America in its day.

Most definitely, Du Bois still believed in battling the Wizard's way.

In January 1905, J. Max Barber's newspaper, *The Voice of the Negro*, ran Du Bois's "Debit and Credit." It accused Booker T. Washington of having bribed black newspapers for favorable coverage in 1904 to the tune of three thousand dollars. J. Max Barber soon lost advertisers. (The Tuskegee Machine at work.)

One of Washington's white fans and financial backers, the imperious Oswald Garrison Villard, gave Du Bois grief for "Debit and Credit." Villard, a Harvard man four years his junior, came from social change-making on one side of the family and money-making on the other. His mother, Fanny, a women's-rights activist, was a daughter of legendary abolitionist William Lloyd Garrison. Oswald's father, Henry, had been a railroad magnate, founding president of what would become General Electric, and owner of the daily *New York Evening Post* and the weekly *Nation*. Oswald Villard had inherited both periodicals. When he took Du Bois to task for "Debit and Credit," he challenged him to back up his accusation with facts for publication in the *New York Evening Post*.

Du Bois was only willing to provide information for Villard's private perusal. The evidence included the claim by an assistant editor of the *Colored American* that this newspaper received five hundred dollars a year from Tuskegee. Du Bois also told

Villard straight up that he despised blacks who sold out their periodicals. On the list was his childhood idol, T. Thomas Fortune, then on his third newspaper, the *New York Age*.

Fortune had become less fierce and brave as his money troubles grew, in part because he lived above his means. He welcomed opportunities to ghostwrite and edit for Washington (speeches, articles, books), more so as his life spiraled out of control. Fortune's other big problem: drinking overmuch.

Villard wasn't moved by anything Du Bois said about Washington or anybody else. What's more, he lectured Du Bois about the company he kept, calling Monroe Trotter "a very dangerous" man.

Trotter was among the dozens of men Du Bois contacted two months later in his call for a conference. It was time for a united front against the Wizard's way.

Sixty guys said that they would attend. Twenty-nine showed, Trotter among them.

The date: July 11–13, 1905.

The place: The Erie Beach Hotel on the Canadian side of Niagara Falls.

The result: a civil-rights organization, the Niagara Movement.

Du Bois and Trotter drafted the Niagara Movement's *Declaration of Principles*, announcing what the group stood for. In a word: Justice—from the black man's right to vote *throughout the nation* to equal opportunity in employment and education.

Until racial justice became a reality, the Niagara Movement was committed to "Agitation," because "persistent manly agitation is the way to liberty, and toward this goal the Niagara Movement has started and asks the co-operation of all men of all races."

The men of Niagara also asked blacks not to be slackers, but to do their duty. At the top of the list: vote. About a half-million black men outside the South hadn't been stripped of that right, and they needed to not take it for granted.

The Niagara Movement was incorporated in January 1906 with thirty-seven-year-old Du Bois its general secretary.

By then, he was also the Man in the Moon, editor in chief of a new magazine: *The Moon Illustrated*

Weekly. The first issue came out in early December 1905. Du Bois's partners were AU grads Edward Simon and Harry Pace, who quit their teaching jobs at Southern schools for the venture.

For about $2,700 (upwards of $60,000 in today's dollars), the trio had purchased a printing plant in Memphis, on Beale Street. Ed Simon ran the shop, handling whatever print jobs they could drum up in addition to putting out *The Moon*. Harry Pace was the magazine's business manager. Keeping his job at AU, Du Bois ran the show editorially.

Few issues of *The Moon* have survived. One is the March 1906 issue. It was dedicated to a founding member of the American Negro Academy, poet Paul Laurence Dunbar, who had died in February. (Du Bois had first met the Dayton, Ohio, native when he was teaching at Wilberforce.)

A late June *Moon* had a heads-up on the second Niagara Movement convention: August 15–19, 1906, at Harper's Ferry, West Virginia. It was at the federal armory there that, in 1859, the white abolitionist John

Superimposed on an image of Niagara Falls, Du Bois (middle row, fourth from left) with other Niagara men, including Clement Morgan, now a lawyer (bottom row, second from left).

Brown had launched what he envisioned as an epic uprising against slavery, for which he was hanged. Du Bois had been commissioned to write a biography of John Brown for the *American Crisis Biographies*, which covered the Civil War, from causes to consequences.

About one hundred people attended the second Niagara Movement convention, held at Storer College, West Virginia's first college for blacks. Attendees included John Hope, president of Atlanta Baptist College for men (to be renamed Morehouse in a few years), and one of Du Bois's best friends.

Women were on the scene this time (as Du Bois had willed and Trotter had resisted). Niagara women included Clement Morgan's wife, Gertrude, and Storer student Mary Clifford, whose father, lawyer J. R. Clifford, headed the West Virginia chapter. During the opening of one session, Mary Clifford recited "Credo."

The only white person to attend was a woman: socialist Mary White Ovington, a New York City social worker and journalist, and granddaughter of an abolitionist (Emeline Ketcham). Ovington first met Du Bois in 1904 when visiting the South, and the two had kept in touch. When she asked if she could attend the convention to cover it for Oswald Villard's *New York Evening Post*, Du Bois said sure.

At the dawn of day three of the convention, August 17, 1906, the Niagara Movement paid tribute to firebrand John Brown. From one of Storer's hilltop halls down to the armory, the men and women of Niagara marched. Barefoot. Silent. Candles in hand.

Some may have sent up prayers for the 25th Infantry, stationed in Brownsville, Texas. This black regiment was in lockup. Because whites had claimed that some of these soldiers had gone on a shoot-'em-up in town. All were being punished because none named the guilty. Justice for the men in the "Brownsville Incident" was another cause the Niagara Movement was to champion.

Du Bois's "Address to the Country," read on the convention's last day, was largely a repeat of the Niagara Movement's *Declaration of Principles*, but it hammered especially hard at education: "We want our children educated. The school system in the country districts of the South is a disgrace and in few towns and cities are the Negro schools what they ought to be.

We want the national government to step in and wipe out illiteracy in the South. Either the United States will destroy ignorance or ignorance will destroy the United States."

The piece closed on a soaring note of hope: "The morning breaks over blood-stained hills. We must not falter, we may not shrink. Above are the everlasting stars."

But *The Moon* was no more. It saw its last shining that summer. Money was the matter.

Du Bois soon faced something more devastating.

Blood-stained hills for real.

EIGHT

"O SILENT GOD, *Thou whose voice afar in mist and mystery hath left our ears a-hungered in these fearful days—"*

September 1906. The start of the poem Du Bois began writing during his anxious journey home from Lowndes County, Alabama. He was doing research there for a census bureau project when word reached him of atrocity in Atlanta.

"Hear us, good Lord!"

In their appeals for white votes, contenders for Georgia's governorship, Hoke Smith and Clarke Howell, had been whipping up fear and loathing for blacks. Then, on Saturday, September 22, several white-owned Atlanta newspapers ran never-substantiated stories of black-on-white crimes, including the rape of white women.

Whites crowded downtown Atlanta that evening.

"We beseech Thee to hear us, good Lord!"

The gathering became a mob ten thousand strong.

"We are not better than our fellows, Lord; we are but weak and human men . . ."

Someone shouted, "Kill the niggers!"

"Have mercy upon us . . ."

Black homes, businesses, and schools were trashed and burned. Black people were clubbed. Stabbed. Strung up on poles. Riddled with bullets. A baby was held up for target practice. A crippled boy beaten to a pulp.

"Red was the midnight."

The terror lasted four days.

When Du Bois reached Atlanta, he found Nina and six-year-old Yolande terrified but unharmed. Still, he got ahold of a double-barreled shotgun—"If a white mob stepped on the campus . . . I would without hesitation have sprayed their guts over the grass."

"Selah!

Done at Atlanta, in the Day of Death, 1906."

These words closed Du Bois's poem: "A Litany of Atlanta," published in the *Independent* in mid-October.

Later that month, Du Bois received a letter from

In profile, courage.

Edwin Seligman, a fellow professor and a leading member of New York City's progressive Jewish community. Seligman told Du Bois that he had been "amazed & disgusted at the happenings in Atlanta. But perhaps I did not realize the horror of it all, until I read your beautiful poem." The recently widowed Seligman hoped that in the wake of the tragedy, Du Bois recognized, as he did, that, "there are really only two things worth living for in this world." One was the love of those near and dear. The other was work organic to one's soul.

Du Bois didn't miss a beat in his whirl of work—completing his Lowndes County study, going on a January–February 1907 speaking tour in the North, mapping out more AU studies, and planning the next Niagara Movement convention. He still hadn't finished his book on John Brown.

That didn't stop him from launching a new magazine, *The Horizon: A Journal of the Color Line.* Yes, *The Moon* had failed, but as historian Herbert Aptheker remarked, for Du Bois "failure existed as an encouragement to renewed effort."

Only this time Du Bois made his magazine a monthly instead of a weekly. He had new business partners, too: the brothers (and Niagara men) F. Morris Murray and F. H. M. Murray. They published the magazine in their print shop (in D.C., then in nearby Alexandria, Virginia, then again in D.C.).

"If the truth must be told, [President] Theodore Roosevelt does not like black folk," Du Bois declared in *The Horizon*'s first issue (January 1907). He was furious about the fate of the men in the Brownsville Incident. President Roosevelt had signed off on the dishonorable discharge of the entire 25th Infantry, killing the careers and pensions of 167 men. (The regiment would be exonerated—in 1970, when all but one of the soldiers were dead.)

And Du Bois didn't like capitalism.

In the February *Horizon* he announced himself a "Socialist-of-the-Path." He wasn't for the abolition of all private property, but he believed that certain industries—the railroads and coal mines, for example— should be "run by the public for the public." He saw in socialism the "one great hope" of blacks and all oppressed people—not the "Get and Grab" ethic of capitalism.

Many of the books Du Bois recommended in *The*

Horizon were by socialists. Example: *War of the Classes* by the white writer Jack London, best known for his novel *The Call of the Wild.*

Du Bois was adamant about blacks buying books. "Buy books. Do not merely read them but buy them, own them, make them yours," he urged in a Spring 1907 *Horizon.* Yes, magazines and newspapers had their place, but "a book is a serious thought-out theme written to live. Therefore buy books. The more books we buy the more books written to our liking will be published for others to buy and ponder. Buy books."

Keep up with other people's plights! he urged, by recommending articles on immigrants, for example, and through briefs on the degradation of blacks in the Belgian Congo and other colonies. Lynchings, voting-rights violations, pitiful public schools were among the domestic issues *The Horizon* kept before its readers.

When the July *Horizon* came out, Du Bois was in Europe, solo, for a little R&R, moving around England, France, and Scotland, a lot by bike. Shortly after he returned, he was in Boston for the third Niagara Movement convention, troubled behind the scenes by a power struggle between him and Trotter.

The September *Horizon* announced that the Niagara Movement had four hundred members in thirty-five states and had "kept up the campaign of agitation for Negro rights."

The October *Horizon* carried a reprint of a letter published in another periodical with a painful reminder of the need for agitation.

> Dear Sir: . . . You ask me of the man that was lynched. He was Pettigrew, and was lynched without being allowed five minutes to tell the facts or to prove himself innocent. With 67 White men about him, well armed, he was shot to death. . . . After he was killed he was dragged on the ground with his feet tied behind a buggy to a place a mile out of town.

Not all news was depressing. "An Essay by a Southern White Boy" was the header Du Bois gave his reprint of an eleven-year-old Alabamian's plea for racial justice.

The Horizon had more readers than *The Moon*, but it was still a struggling operation. So was the Niagara Movement. The turnout for the 1908 convention in Oberlin, Ohio, was low. Some members bailed because raising money and peoplepower to maintain a chapter was tough. Others caved in to pressure from the Tuskegee Machine. Plum jobs were dangled to keep quiet. Good jobs were threatened if people spoke up.

Du Bois kept up a good front in the annual address: "The Niagara Movement at its fourth annual meeting congratulates ten million Negro Americans, on their unparalleled opportunity to lead the greatest moral battle of modern times—the fight for the abolition of the color line."

There was a word about self-defense.

"We say to our own: Obey the law, defend no crime, conceal no criminal, seek no quarrel: but arm yourselves, and when the mob invades your home, shoot, and shoot to kill."

Blacks had been recently attacked in Springfield, Illinois, where Abraham Lincoln had spent most of his life, and in the year of the centennial of his birth.

"Curse the day that Lincoln freed the niggers!" was one battle cry of whites on the warpath after a married white woman falsely accused a black man of assaulting her to cover up the fact that her white boyfriend had beat her up.

"Was I doing anything for the fundamental cause of the race's condition?" Mary White Ovington agonized as she read an article about Springfield, "Race War in the North," by another white socialist William English Walling.

"Who realizes the seriousness of the situation, and what large and powerful body of citizens is ready to come to" the aid of black folks? Walling asked.

Ovington reached out to him, ready to create just such a group. The like-minded included Lillian Wald, founder of a New York City social service center for the poor, the Henry Street Settlement House, and millionaire John Milholland, whose Constitution League had come to the defense of the 25th Infantry (and whose daughter Inez became a fiery suffragist). Also on board, Oswald Villard, semi-nemesis of Du Bois.

Both Villard and Du Bois were among the three hundred people at a spring 1909 conference in downtown Manhattan. Du Bois remembered this mostly white event as "a visible bursting into action of long gathering thought and brooding." This thought and brooding evolved into the National Association for the Advancement of Colored People (NAACP).

The NAACP's founding white members weren't

all gentiles like Ovington, Walling, Milholland, and Villard. Many were Jews. In addition to Lillian Wald, they included the Spingarn brothers: Arthur, a lawyer, and Joel, a former college professor, whose independently wealthy wife, Amy, would also be involved.

Ida B. Wells-Barnett was also a founding member. She had joined the Niagara Movement in 1909, the year of its last convention (in Sea Isle City, New Jersey). Du Bois hoped that the entire Niagara Movement would fold into the NAACP. Trotter was among those who said, Oh, no. He couldn't see black progress being charted by a majority-white organization. Trotter was still up for fighting for every right with all his might, but he would go his own way.

Shortsighted, thought Du Bois, who became so much more than a member of the NAACP.

NINE

"THE OBJECT OF this publication is to set forth those facts and arguments which show the danger of race prejudice, particularly as manifested to-day toward colored people," Du Bois explained in the first issue (November 1910) of the NAACP's monthly magazine, *The Crisis*.

Its title was inspired by a favorite poem of Ovington's, "The Present Crisis" by white abolitionist James Russell Lowell, with the challenge:

> *Once to every man and nation comes the moment to*
> *decide,*
> *In the strife of Truth with Falsehood, for the good or*
> *evil side.*

When the NAACP offered Du Bois the job as

THE CRISIS

A RECORD OF THE DARKER RACES

Volume One NOVEMBER, 1910 Number One

Edited by W. E. BURGHARDT DU BOIS, with the co-operation of Oswald Garrison Villard, J. Max Barber, Charles Edward Russell, Kelly Miller, W. S. Braithwaite and M. D. Maclean.

CONTENTS

PUBLISHED MONTHLY BY THE

National Association for the Advancement of Colored People

AT TWENTY VESEY STREET   NEW YORK CITY

ONE DOLLAR A YEAR   TEN CENTS A COPY

Cover of the premiere issue of Du Bois's new magazine.

director of publicity and research at a yearly salary of $2,500, he felt that he could better fight for the good with the NAACP than at AU. So in August 1910, forty-two-year-old Du Bois packed his bags for New York City, leaving Nina and ten-year-old Yolande behind while he got settled.

Thanks to Oswald Villard, the NAACP had free office space in lower Manhattan at 20 Vesey Street, headquarters of his periodicals. As for Du Bois's *Horizon*, its last issue was July 1910.

The first issue of *The Crisis* had a printing of 1,000. By July 1911, its circulation was 15,000. By the end of 1915, it had climbed to more than 36,000.

The Crisis was reflective of its editor's wide-angle mind. International news ranged from archeological digs in Ethiopia to Italy's invasion of Tripoli. The column "What to Read" spotlighted books as different as *Three Lives* by white writer Gertrude Stein and *The Soul of the Indian* by Sioux physician Charles Eastman.

Other early columns included "Men of the Month," "Talks About Women," "Along the Color Line" (on hopes and happenings in black America), and "The

Burden" (on racist events and sentiments). *The Crisis* was also a feast for the eyes, filled with photographs, especially of Talented Tenthers.

By late 1915, when his magazine was on the verge of needing no subsidy from the NAACP, running *The Crisis* wasn't the only thing keeping Du Bois busy.

He had lectured around the U.S. to both black and white audiences, promoting the NAACP and *The Crisis*. In June 1911, Du Bois had been to England for the Universal Races Congress, a multiracial, multinational condemnation of the color line and celebration of humankind. There, he read his poem "A Hymn to the Peoples" with its cry "Save us, World-Spirit, from our lesser selves!" and its call for no more war, no more hate, but a "Humanity divine!"

Jamaica, West Indies. Du Bois had been there, too, in the summer of 1915. No work, no conference. Vacation this time. He found this British colony with its "mass of gray, green mountains" a "most amazing island" with the "maddest, wildest, and wettest of rains." He did lots of sightseeing, and was officially *seen* at a reception in his honor, courtesy of the island's royal governor. During the social, Du Bois met a very dark-skinned man with penetrating eyes and a passion for his island's independence. This printer by trade also hungered for a united black world. For this cause, he had started an organization that would take the name Universal Negro Improvement Association (UNIA). His name: Marcus Mosiah Garvey. He hoped for some one-on-one time with Du Bois, but that never happened.

By late 1915, Du Bois had also put out a waterfall of words—and not just articles.

His biography of John Brown had been published in fall 1909. In 1911 came his first novel, *The Quest of the Silver Fleece*, set mainly in a fictional Alabama town, Toomsville, where most blacks are sharecroppers. It's also where a gutsy white New Englander, Miss Smith, struggles to maintain her school for blacks. One of her students is the straight-arrow striver Bles Alwyn. Another is the wild child Zora, daughter of a witch and denizen of the swamp. To everyone's amazement, Zora becomes a great leader, creating a socialist black enclave in Toomsville.

Drama. Du Bois had also tackled that art form. For the fiftieth anniversary of the Emancipation

Proclamation, he wrote a pageant, *The People of Peoples and Their Gifts*, a celebration of people of African descent from prehistoric times to his own. In fall 1913, the pageant was performed at an armory in New York City during its Emancipation Proclamation Expo. It was later produced in Philadelphia, D.C., and L.A. By then, Du Bois had renamed it *The Star of Ethiopia*.

"Africa" was the title of a chapter in Du Bois's *The Negro*, a history of Africa and black America, published in May 1915.

In November, the man once regarded as *the* Negro in the U.S. died. Du Bois didn't crow when he wrote of Booker T. Washington's passing in *The Crisis*. He called him the "most distinguished" Southern man since the Civil War. After praising Washington for promoting black economic development, Du Bois went on to blame him for the same things he always had.

Before Washington died, his popularity among blacks was in decline as Du Bois's rose, chiefly because of *The Crisis*. In many black homes it was second only to the Bible. One woman told Du Bois that the December 1915 issue went with her father to the grave. As the man lay dying, he had hoped to live long enough to read that issue.

✻ ✻ ✻

The year 1915 was also the year of D. W. Griffith's film *Birth of a Nation*, with its distorted portrait of Reconstruction. The KKK was noble, said the film. The black man was depicted "either as an ignorant fool, a vicious rapist, a venal or unscrupulous politician or a faithful but doddering idiot," Du Bois fumed in *The Crisis.*

The NAACP's national campaign against *Birth of a Nation* included mobilizing people to picket theaters that showed the film so offensive to blacks— and hazardous to their lives. Some whites left movie theaters seeing red and out for black blood. The KKK used the film as a recruiting tool. Its membership soared.

So did the NAACP's. More people joined because of its campaign against *Birth of a Nation* than had joined for its other initiatives, such as publicizing lynchings and giving legal aid to blacks falsely accused of crimes or guilty but serving undue sentences.

The NAACP's first U.S. Supreme Court victory also came in 1915, in June, in the case *Guinn v. United States,* masterminded by the white lawyer Moorfield Storey, the NAACP's president since its inception. In

Guinn v. United States, the U.S. Supreme Court struck down Oklahoma's "grandfather clause." The victory strengthened the NAACP's resolve to work against Jim Crow through the courts.

Still, many blacks looked askance at the NAACP. Except for Du Bois, its officers were white. Makes sense, some said, because they were mostly whites with money, connections to money, and clout in some quarters.

Du Bois had no problem with the makeup of the NAACP leadership per se, but he had a big problem with some fellow officers, especially Oswald Villard, its second chairman of the board of directors. (William Walling was its first.)

Villard had come a ways since his days of unqualified support for the Wizard, but he had a long way to go in terms of truly seeing blacks as equals. He was still paternalistic, still condescending. He got on Du Bois's last nerve with his insistence that *The Crisis* report on black criminals so long as it reported on blacks murdered by white mobs. At a time when so many white-owned periodicals rarely reported on blacks as anything *but* criminals, what a racist and backward idea, thought Du Bois.

Du Bois largely ignored Villard. He didn't think he had to answer to anyone. *He* made the magazine a success. Most of the board didn't want to tamper with success.

Villard resigned as chairman in 1914, and the NAACP soon moved from 20 Vesey Street up to 70 Fifth Avenue. (Villard quit the NAACP in 1916.)

The board's new chair was Joel Spingarn, whom Du Bois liked and admired (and the feeling was mutual). Shortly after Spingarn took office, he sent Du Bois a letter in which he reaffirmed his respect and support, but said that he found Du Bois often stubborn, not a team player, and prickly.

Du Bois defended some of his prickliness, but also copped to some of Spingarn's criticism: "I do not doubt in the least but that my temperament is a difficult one to endure."

His family affairs were difficult, too.

TEN

"ABOVE ALL REMEMBER, dear, that you have a great opportunity. You are in one of the world's best schools. . . . Deserve it, then. Study, do your work."

October 29, 1914, from a letter to teenaged Yolande, signed "Lovingly yours, Papa."

When Du Bois's wife and daughter joined him in New York, the family lived in a rented house in the north Bronx. Nina and Yolande might as well have been in Atlanta still. Lovingly Papa was hardly home.

Nina had never played a role in her husband's great ambitions. Now she was becoming the great invisible.

The marriage had begun to fray years ago. Burghardt's death left a rift. Yolande's birth didn't bridge the gap, but it left Nina obsessive about keeping

Yolande as a young lady.

home and daughter germ-free. She fretted over Yolande's every ache, every scratch, even more after Yolande had an appendectomy at age eight.

Nina's Will was more obsessed with their daughter's mind. He wanted her to be a little him, a little busy-brained genius. That wasn't Yolande. She was her era's equivalent of a couch potato, overeating and averse to physical activity. What her father described as her "very slovenly" command of the English language was equally vexing. The fix: send Yolande to a progressive British boarding school (which put great stock in physical activity). The school was Bedales, in the Hampshire County village of Steep. Its students included two children of the socialist Ramsay MacDonald, head of the Labour Party (and future prime minister of the United Kingdom). Du Bois first met him in 1911 at the Universal Races Congress. Having MacDonald as a reference helped Du Bois get Yolande into Bedales.

Where Yolande went, went Nina. They reached England in October 1914, shortly before Yolande's fourteenth birthday.

In that letter urging Yolande to do her utmost in school, Lovingly Papa challenged her to embrace "the ability to do, the will to conquer, the determination to understand and know this great wonderful, curious world." He commanded her to read some "good, heavy, serious books just for the discipline."

Yolande couldn't bear the pressure to know the world and didn't care for heavy books. "I can't help it if I'm stupid," she would write her father.

Nina didn't like England. Not the food. Not the weather. And certainly not the stress of being in a foreign land when it was at war—a war that would be called the Great War, and later World War I.

Its surface cause was the murder of royals: Franz Ferdinand, heir to the throne of the Austro-Hungarian Empire, and his wife, Sophie. On June 28, 1914, a Serbian man shot them dead, in Sarajevo, capital of Bosnia-Herzegovina, largely inhabited by Serbians but ruled by Austria-Hungary. Holding Serbia responsible for the assassinations, Austria-Hungary declared war on that nation.

Austria-Hungary's allies would include Bulgaria, the Ottoman Empire, and Germany. Serbia's: Canada, Russia, France, Italy, eventually the U.S., and Great Britain, which had entered the war two months before Du Bois sent his wife and daughter to England.

What was he thinking?

What he thought Bedales would do for Yolande never happened. Her attitude and academic performance left a lot to be desired. Bedales decided it was not the school for her. Mother and daughter were back in the U.S. in August 1916. (Yolande would attend Girls' High in Brooklyn, New York, where the Du Boises would soon move. After high school, she'd attend Fisk.)

When Nina and Yolande returned from England in 1916, Nina had started referring to her daughter as "Ouchie" because of the girl's frequent aches and ails, real and phantom.

A few months after his family returned home, Lovingly Papa was under the knife at Manhattan's St. Luke's Hospital. He had been plagued by kidney stones. Now his left kidney had to be removed.

Legions of black Americans held their breath.

"Your illness has made us realize how much we owe to you, and that to lose you would mean a greater calamity to the race than we can express," wrote NAACPer Carrie Clifford on January 20, 1917. Du

Bois was "indispensable." So, please, Clifford urged, please refrain from the "over-working as you have done."

Du Bois left the hospital on January 22 and was doing well, he informed Clifford a few days later. "I am glad to learn how important I am," he added.

Stop "over-working"?

"MR. PRESIDENT, WHY NOT MAKE AMERICA SAFE FOR DEMOCRACY?" asked banners in an NAACP landmark march on July 28, 1917.

Some eight thousand souls marched down New York City's Fifth Avenue.

Men in dark suits.

Women and children in white.

All of them silent.

Du Bois in the forefront.

He had recently returned from a fact-finding mission in East St. Louis, Illinois, where white resentment over blacks getting jobs at local factories and rumors of a black plan to go on a rampage resulted in another bloody horror, another "red was the midnight."

Thus, the NAACP's Silent March.

Thus, the question, "MR. PRESIDENT, WHY NOT MAKE AMERICA SAFE FOR DEMOCRACY?"

Mr. President was Woodrow Wilson. Making the *world* safe for democracy was why, Wilson had said, the nation had to enter the European war, and that's what the U.S. had done, in April 1917.

Du Bois hated war in general and Woodrow Wilson in particular. Back in 1912, when Wilson was running for president, Du Bois had rallied blacks to vote for him. Wilson had vowed to be "President of all the people"; he had said that he wanted "justice done to the colored people in every matter."

Once president, Wilson made the federal government—with all its bureaus and offices—Jim Crow, from eating facilities to restrooms. He also jettisoned most black civil servants.

Despite his feelings about war and Wilson, Du Bois ended up urging blacks to rally 'round the flag. He was up for a compromise.

Black people: Support the war effort!

White people: Do the right thing by black folks after the war, okay?

"Let us not hesitate," Du Bois told blacks in "Close Ranks," his July 1918 *Crisis* editorial. "Let us, while this war lasts, forget our special grievances and close our ranks shoulder to shoulder with our own white fellow citizens and the allied nations that are fighting for democracy."

Forget about lynching? Segregation? Voting rights? Forget about East St. Louis?

The radical black press blasted Du Bois for "Close Ranks," especially after people learned that he was up for a captaincy in military intelligence (thanks to Joel Spingarn, himself to be an army officer).

The hue and cry soon died down. In late July, Du Bois's captaincy was withdrawn. In November, World War I was over.

And now what? After almost 21 million lives, military and civilian, lost, and other millions scarred and maimed.

In early December 1918, fifty-year-old Du Bois sailed to Europe to cover the Paris Peace Conference. It would result in the Treaty of Versailles, which would give rise to the need for new maps. For one, Austria-Hungary would be gone, its territories to become independent nations (Czechoslovakia, among them). Germany would be stripped of territory in Europe (France got Alsace-Lorraine, for example) and all its colonies, including those in Africa. But there would be no independence for black folks. German South West Africa (present-day Namibia), for example, became part of the British Empire.

In addition to covering the peace talks, Du Bois also gathered information on the heroics of black soldiers and the horrible treatment some had received at white American hands. Of the roughly four million Americans who served in their nation's Jim Crow military, about 380,000 were black. The majority of them (some 200,000) served overseas as stevedores and laborers. About 40,000 were in combat, with the 369th regiment—the "Harlem Hellfighters"—earning high honors for valor while fighting alongside French troops. This, after white American troops in France refused to close ranks with them shoulder to shoulder.

Du Bois had a new great ambition: a major book on the war, *The Black Man and the Wounded World*. (He would write several articles on blacks in World War I, but his big book would remain on eternal hold.)

For wounded Africa, Du Bois scrambled to assemble

another black solidarity conference, called a Pan-African Congress. Held in late February 1919 at Paris's Grand Hotel, its sixty delegates included Haitians, Liberians, an Algerian, and more than a dozen Americans. The upshot was yet another call for humane treatment of Africans living under European rule.

Europe yawned.

As Du Bois told *Crisis* readers, European powers weren't truly interested in the "spread of European civilization" as they claimed, but in "a field for exploitation. They covet the raw materials,—ivory, diamonds, copper and rubber in which the land abounds, and even more do they covet cheap native labor to mine and produce these things. Greed,—naked, pitiless lust for wealth and power, lie back of all of Europe's interest in Africa and the white world knows it and is not ashamed."

When Du Bois returned to the U.S., he was in a fighting mood.

ELEVEN

"WE ARE RETURNING FROM WAR! *The Crisis* and tens of thousands of black men were drafted into a great struggle," Du Bois declared in his May 1919 editorial, "Returning Soldiers."

Du Bois became the voice of all blacks who had fought "for America and her highest ideals" and "in far-off hope" for racial justice.

"We sing: This country of ours, despite all its better souls have done and dreamed, is yet a shameful land."

Shameful because "It *lynches*. . . . It *disfranchises*. . . . It encourages *ignorance*. . . . Its *steals* from us. . . . It *insults* us."

Blacks would be "cowards and jackasses if now that that war is over, we do not marshal every ounce of our brain and brawn to fight a sterner, longer, more unbending battle against the forces of hell in our own land." He began his wrap with this:

> We *return.*
> We *return from fighting.*
> We *return fighting.*

Nonviolent combat, that is; however, events soon compelled Du Bois to call for physical fighting—*back*, echoing the energy of Claude McKay's sonnet "If We Must Die," which ends:

> *Like men we'll face the murderous, cowardly pack,*
> *Pressed to the wall, dying but fighting back!*

Du Bois and McKay were responding to a rash of race riots in 1919 in more than twenty cities, North and South. The summer months were the bloodiest.

Red Summer.

Bloody because of resentment over black job gains during the wartime economic boom and because of the ever-increasing migration to the North of blacks—committing the "crime," in some white eyes, of "not knowing their place." Also, more blacks, especially veterans, refused to bow and scrape before whites. If attacked—fight *back*.

White social worker John Shillady, the NAACP's executive secretary—essentially its CEO—couldn't fight back in Austin, Texas. Shillady was there in August 1919 because authorities were bullying the city's NAACP branch, looking for a reason to shut it down. To shut down Shillady, a pack of white men, a judge among them, jumped him. "The haters of black folk beat him and maltreated him and scarred him like a dog because he tried to talk quiet reason to Texas," roared Du Bois in *The Crisis*.

Shillady soon resigned. The NAACP's next executive secretary was a black man: AU grad James Weldon Johnson, a writer and more.

Johnson had been serving as the NAACP's field secretary, traveling around the nation to fortify and develop branches. Thanks in large part to him, by 1919 the NAACP had about ninety thousand members in roughly three hundred branches. Johnson had long since given black America the song that became its anthem, "Lift Every Voice and Sing." He also coined the term "Red Summer."

The "Red Scare" was also raging in 1919. Red as in Communist.

Red was the banner color of the political party that ended up in control of Russia after the Czarist regime was toppled during World War I. Russia became the Russian Soviet Socialist Republic. (*Soviet* is Russian for council.) The revolution's leader, Vladimir Lenin, changed the party's name from Bolshevik ("majority") to Communist, because its ultimate goal for the nation was communism. Think extreme socialism.

Communism calls for no government and no private property. Instead, a nation's resources are to be managed by the people collectively, for the making of a society with no upper class, no middle class, no lower class, no underclass. Until people were ready for such a society, the Communist Party would rule.

As Russia went, so went other territories once part of the Russian Empire (in Western Europe, the Caucasus, and Central Asia). Life was turned upside down. Many of the high and mighty lost their lives, their property, or both. Clerics were also persecuted and killed, because religion was condemned. All this was the price of creating a utopia, many communists maintained.

Down with capitalism! radical Americans cried, inspired by the Russian Revolution—and some promoted violence.

Ka-boom! Ka-boom! Ka-boom! Homes and offices of bankers, industrialists, politicians, judges, and other representatives of the power structure were bombed, resulting in injuries, and in some cases, deaths.

The government fought back, calling on all "good" Americans to denounce radicals—revile Reds, with communists, socialists, and anarchists lumped together.

Left-wingers lost friends, lost jobs, and some lost their lives at the hands of mobs. Still others lost their liberty and spent years in prison—or, if noncitizens, were deported.

This roundup of radicals became known as the Palmer Raids after the man who authorized them: U.S. Attorney General A. Mitchell Palmer. His home had been ka-boomed in June 1919.

Micromanaging the Palmer Raids was J. Edgar Hoover, future chief of the FBI. In 1919, Hoover produced the report "Radicalism and Sedition Among Negroes as Reflected in their Publications." This watch list included *The Crisis*, which had a circulation of 100,000 by spring 1919.

Later that year, Du Bois announced the coming of a new magazine: *The Brownies' Book*, a monthly for children. *The Crisis* already had an annual children's issue (October), but Du Bois wanted black children to have more. In January 1920 they did.

The magazine was a joint venture of Du Bois and Augustus Dill. Dill had studied under Du Bois at AU, worked with him on several AU studies, gone on to become a Harvard man, and been business manager for *The Crisis* since 1913.

Jessie Fauset was the literary editor of *The Brownies' Book*. Since her thank-you letter to Du Bois for *Souls*—"It hurt you to write that book, didn't it?"—Fauset had graduated from Cornell Phi Beta Kappa, taught French and Latin at D.C.'s M Street School, studied at the Sorbonne in Paris, and earned a master's degree in French at the University of Pennsylvania in 1919. Shortly after that, this Talented Tenther became literary editor for *The Crisis*. Fauset didn't work on both magazines for long. *The Brownies' Book* only lasted two years.

✳ ✳ ✳

By the time *The Brownies' Book* folded in late 1921, Du Bois had another book out, *Darkwater: Voices from Within the Veil* (1920), a collection of fiction, nonfiction, and poetry, considered a sequel to *Souls*.

Like that 1903 book, some of *Darkwater* had already appeared in periodicals. The book's first main piece is "Credo." Next, "The Shadow of Years," a mini memoir, in which Du Bois presents his childhood as a little lovelier than it was. He claims, for example, that his father had tried to reunite with the family, only his mother no longer trusted him.

Other essays assailed colonialism, the notion of white supremacy, and other evils. "The Damnation of Women" cheers for women, with a special tribute to the struggles, strivings, and strengths of black women, from obscure souls such as Du Bois's Dear Mam to legends like Sojourner Truth.

Du Bois had written several articles in support of the women's-suffrage movement. He had also devoted two issues of *The Crisis* to this cause, victorious the year *Darkwater* appeared. In August 1920 women gained the national vote (the Nineteenth Amendment). "The Damnation of Women" was yet another

June 1920, Atlanta: Receiving the NAACP's highest honor, the Spingarn Award, given annually to a black person of outstanding achievement.

call for women to be seen as, yes, different from but not inferior to men. Du Bois revered women of drive and ambition: women like his characters Ella Boyd (*Tom Brown at Fisk*) and Zora (*The Quest of the Silver Fleece*)—women who were everything his wife was not. Du Bois dedicated *Darkwater* to Nina, but when he wrote of their early life together in "The Shadow of Years," he gave her short shrift, summing her up as "a slip of a girl, beautifully dark-eyed and thorough and good as a German housewife."

Darkwater ends with "A Hymn to the Peoples," the

poem Du Bois read at the Universal Races Congress in England back in 1911—*"Save us, World-Spirit, from our lesser selves!"*

Du Bois had been to Europe again, in late summer 1921, for the second Pan-African Congress, which started in Paris, continued in London, and closed in Brussels. This congress had more than one hundred delegates: more than thirty from the U.S., more than forty from Africa. And this time, the message to the world was: either end racial discrimination in colonial Africa or create a new black-run African state.

Du Bois's closest companion during this trip was Jessie Fauset, fan turned colleague turned lover. Though miserable in his marriage, divorce was not an option for Du Bois. Divorce carried more of a stigma back then, and Du Bois had an image to maintain.

Also with Du Bois and Fauset at the 1921 Pan-African Congress was Walter White, the NAACP's assistant executive secretary since 1918. This AU grad (1916) and cofounder of the NAACP's Atlanta branch was thirteen at the time of the 1906 pogrom in Atlanta. After living through that, the very light-skinned, blond-haired, blue-eyed black man could have opted to reinvent himself and live as a white man. He did some passing, but mostly when on NAACP business, investigating mob violence against blacks.

Though White attended the Pan-African Congress, he did so more out of curiosity. He didn't have Du Bois's commitment to Pan-Africanism.

Du Bois wasn't the only black man in the U.S. calling for black solidarity. Most notably there was the man he had met briefly in Jamaica, Marcus Garvey. He had been in New York City since 1916 and his UNIA—with its call for black pride, black separatism, and black rule of sub-Saharan Africa—had millions of members around the U.S., in Africa, the Caribbean, and elsewhere.

Most Garveyites were not Talented Tenthers, but workaday folks (domestic workers and laborers, for example). UNIA also attracted a Baptist preacher in Omaha, Nebraska, Earl Little, whose son Malcolm would one day replace his surname with an X.

Other early Garvey supporters included Ida B. Wells-Barnett (who had quit the NAACP). Another was hair-care millionaire and NAACP supporter

Madame C. J. Walker. She financed the startup of Garvey's newspaper, *The Negro World*, for which T. Thomas Fortune, still on the skids, worked for a time. Walker also fronted the money for UNIA headquarters, Liberty Hall, in Harlem, where Garvey held massive rallies and managed various business ventures. The best known was a shipping company, the Black Star line.

UNIA—the largest black mass movement yet seen—was a threat to the NAACP. By calling for black separatism, it gave comfort to white separatists, thus cramping the NAACP crusade to end Jim Crow. UNIA was also pulling potential members, along with dues dollars, from the NAACP. (The National Urban League, founded in 1911, was also giving the NAACP competition.)

Du Bois cringed at Garvey's penchant for pomp and pageantry: the parades in which Garveyites marched in military uniforms, the titles Garvey gave his lieutenants (Knights of the Nile, for example) and himself (Provisional President of Africa). Also there was UNIA's flag for the black world, a tri-color—red (for blood), black (for the people), green (for the lush lands of Africa).

Du Bois simply couldn't appreciate the appeal and pride-boosting power of such to the souls of many black folks. As for Garvey's call for millions of black Americans to immigrate to Liberia—ridiculous! thought Du Bois.

In one issue of *The Crisis*, Du Bois's litany of Garvey's "very serious defects" included being "dictatorial, domineering, inordinately vain," and having "absolutely no business sense, no *flair* for real organization."

Who was Du Bois to talk about somebody having no business sense? Garvey countered in *The Negro World*. Hadn't *The Moon* and *The Horizon* flopped? Hadn't the Niagara Movement fizzled? "It was not until a few Boston and New York philanthropists took Dr. Du Bois under their aegis and threw around him the prestige of their wealth and fame that he was able to make *The Crisis* and the NAACP go."

Du Bois was a snob, Garvey also charged: "He only appreciates one type of men, and that is the cultured, refined type which lingers around universities and attends pink tea affairs."

Du Bois soon shot back that Garvey was a "little,

fat, black man; ugly, but with intelligent eyes and a big head."

Garvey's response: "Now, what does Du Bois mean by ugly?" Dark-skinned Garvey called light-skinned Du Bois "a monstrosity."

In the May 1924 *Crisis*, Du Bois proclaimed Garvey "the most dangerous enemy of the Negro race in America and in the world. He is either a lunatic or a traitor."

At the time, Garvey was out on bail pending the appeal of his conviction for what many consider a bogus charge of mail fraud. In February 1925, Garvey's conviction was upheld; he began serving a five-year sentence in an Atlanta prison. In November 1927, President Calvin Coolidge commuted his sentence, and Garvey was deported to Jamaica, as Du Bois and other black activists had urged.

By then Du Bois had been a soul in motion as usual.

Writing.

Articles galore for *The Crisis* and other outlets.

At least two books: *The Gifts of Black Folk* (1924), a history of black contributions to the U.S.; and the novel *Dark Princess* (1928), about the union of a Southern-born black man and an East Indian princess who tosses aside her privilege to cast her lot in with oppressed people of color.

Dark Princess was in part Du Bois's response to the upsurge in the publication and production of art, literary to visual, by blacks: the phenomenon with a catchy but misbegotten name "Harlem Renaissance." (It was not limited to Harlem and was more of a black-arts birth than a rebirth.)

At first, Du Bois was glad to see white publishers and producers bringing black artistry into wider view. He was a big booster of black artists in *The Crisis*. That's why he had Fauset as literary editor, so black writers could have an outlet. (One of her best finds had been Langston Hughes, whom Fauset first published in *The Brownies' Book*, then in *The Crisis*.)

Many a *Crisis* cover was a drawing or painting by a black artist. In 1924, *The Crisis* had launched an arts competition in which winning writers and visual artists received cash prizes. Prize-winning plays were performed by the Krigwa Players, a Harlem theater troupe Du Bois cofounded. (Krigwa was originally

Crigwa, for Crisis Guild of Writers and Artists.)

Du Bois soured on the so-called Harlem Renaissance, because he felt that many works presented blacks in a terrible light. He couldn't stomach novels that featured black prostitutes, gamblers, and crooks, for example. For blacks to write or paint or choreograph whatever they felt like with no regard to how it might help or hinder the race was stupid, Du Bois thought. He said as much at an NAACP conference in Chicago: "I do not care a damn for any art that is not used for propaganda"—that is material that advances a cause. Propaganda like his *Dark Princess*, with its call for people of color around the world to unite!

Traveling. Du Bois had been in Europe again, in late 1923, for the third Pan-African Congress, which began in London and ended in Lisbon. When he left Portugal, he went to a place about which he had written but which he had never seen.

Africa.

TWELVE

"WHEN SHALL I FORGET the night I first set foot on African soil? The moon was at the full and the waters of the Atlantic lay like a lake."

Du Bois was on official business, representing President Coolidge at the inauguration ceremonies for Liberia's new president, Charles King. Du Bois was quite proud of his title—something Marcus Garvey might have envied: "Envoy Extraordinary and Minister Plenipotentiary to Liberia."

Du Bois had an old friend to thank for the appointment: William Lewis, a student at Amherst College when Du Bois was at Harvard. Lewis had gone on to Harvard Law School, served as the first black assistant U.S. attorney general, then become a bigwig in the Republican Party. (And President Coolidge was a Republican.)

Du Bois's precious memories of Liberia included a Christmas Day banquet in the home of a senator, on an estate outside the capital, Monrovia. He also enjoyed a mini-safari. Then, on New Year's Day, 1924, dressed to the nines (from top hat to tails), when he addressed President King, Du Bois made his sentiments Coolidge's. He assured King that the U.S. government truly cared about his country.

When Du Bois left Liberia, he visited Sierra Leone, Guinea, and Senegal, never knowing if his feet touched ground for which that ancestor—"Do bana coba, gene me, gene me!"—had pined.

Du Bois rhapsodized about Africa for *The Crisis*, remarking on how what he saw of the continent was behind the West (technologically, for example) but stressing the ways in which it was more sublime (less hustle and bustle, less materialism). He also went mystical, calling Africa a place where "the Spirit longs to die."

By the time Garvey was deported, Du Bois had also been to the Union of Soviet Socialist Republics (USSR, also known as the Soviet Union). Formed in 1922, the USSR was a federation of post–Russian Revolution states that were once a part of the Russian empire. When Du Bois went to the USSR as its guest in 1926, the republics included Belarus, the Ukraine, Uzbekistan, and, of course, Russia, the seat of power, and where Du Bois spent most of his time during his two-month stay.

The USSR was in bad shape: poor, with millions of war-wounded and a crumbling infrastructure—"Yet, there lay an unforgettable spirit upon the land . . . determined to go forward and establish a government of men, such as the world had never seen," Du Bois later maintained.

He didn't have to travel far at all for the fourth Pan-African Congress, in August 1927. It was held in Harlem, where the Du Boises had been living for a few years by then. They would soon make their Harlem home in the Dunbar Apartments, the Big Apple's first co-op development for blacks. For Du Bois one apartment wouldn't do. Space! More space! He managed to get two apartments combined.

The Du Boises moved into the Dunbar Apartments in early 1928, shortly before Du Bois turned sixty. By then, Joel and Arthur Spingarn had spearheaded a fund-raising campaign to purchase for Du Bois his

Grandpa Othello and Grandma Sarah's homeplace in Great Barrington.

Happy birthday, W. E. B.!

He began making plans to renovate the place for use as a vacation home. The wrought-iron shovel he had taken with him to Fisk some forty years earlier had been lost along the way, but he still had those tongs from his grandparents' fireplace. (He also still had that first major purchase he had made as a teen, the five-volume *History of England.*)

A few months after Du Bois turned sixty, his article "So The Girl Marries" ran in *The Crisis.* It was about Yolande's marriage to the famous poet Countee Cullen. Equally important to Du Bois, Cullen had a master's degree from Harvard. Plus, his parents were pillars of the Harlem community: Pastor and First Lady of Salem Methodist Episcopal Church. That's where Yolande and Countee were married on April 9, 1928.

Yolande wanted a big wedding, and Lovingly Papa had done everything but steal to give her what she wanted:

A wedding party of thirty-plus: women in silk and satin, men in cutaway coats.

Fifteen hundred witnesses (a third of whom Du Bois would feed at the reception).

Outside the church, a crowd of a thousand. For Harlem's Talented Tenthers it was *the* social event of the year.

"Why should there have been so much of pomp and ceremony—flowers and carriages and silk hats; wedding cake and wedding music?" Du Bois asked in his *Crisis* article. Answer: "It must be as this soul wills. The Girl wills this. So the Girl marries."

The marriage was over within a year. Countee Cullen was gay.

While Yolande's marriage was tanking so was the U.S.—and world—economy. In October 1929, the stock market crashed, the tipping point into the Great Depression. Banks would fail and life savings vanish. Businesses would be shuttered, and many millions of Americans would lose their jobs—factory workers, clerks, accountants, police officers, teachers.

Du Bois still had a job. He also had money problems. Beginning in 1930 he had two rents to pay: the double Dunbar apartment and a house in Baltimore, where Nina and Yolande lived. After her divorce from Countee Cullen, Yolande became a high-school teacher in Baltimore. Again, where Yolande went, went Nina.

Du Bois's outlays increased when the Girl got married again in September 1931, to Arnett Williams. Williams had dropped out of Lincoln University in Pennsylvania and was attending a night school operating in the school where Yolande worked. Du Bois insisted that Arnett return to Lincoln and laid out money for his son-in-law's tuition.

In October 1932, the chaotic family had another mouth to feed, one Du Bois could hardly begrudge—a granddaughter: Yolande Du Bois Williams. The family would call her Baby Du Bois.

With Arnett in Pennsylvania, Yolande and Nina were soon back in New York and in the double Dunbar apartment. When Yolande began taking classes at Columbia University's Teachers College, Nina happily took on more responsibility for the care of Baby Du Bois.

Papa Du Bois soon flew the coop.

In late 1932, a visiting professorship at AU was on his horizon. His friend John Hope was now its president. The money was good: two thousand bucks. More important, Du Bois could sorely use some distance from the NAACP, for *The Crisis* was in crisis.

The NAACP wasn't Depression-proof. Membership was down to about twenty thousand. There was much belt-tightening to do. The man doing it was Walter White, now executive secretary. White wanted to husband most of the NAACP's resources for legal challenges against racial injustice.

There was talk of doing away with *The Crisis*. Circulation had dropped to around 25,000. The magazine was no longer self-supporting. Plus, Du Bois's radical thinking rankled Walter White. In *The Crisis* and elsewhere, Du Bois steadily praised the USSR. He also wanted the NAACP to back off the fight against Jim Crow and devote more energy to strategies for black economic development.

As the saying goes, when white America gets a cold, black America gets pneumonia. By 1933, when roughly 25 percent of white workers were unemployed, the figure was about 50 percent for blacks. Hard times called for something new, Du Bois believed.

He and White were oil and water, as was the case with White's second in command and also a black man: career journalist Roy Wilkins. Along with being assistant executive secretary, Roy Wilkins would serve as managing editor of *The Crisis*, handling the day-to-day at 69 Fifth Avenue (the NAACP HQ since late 1930) while Du Bois was on sabbatical at AU. *The Crisis* was still Du Bois's baby. His salary was reduced to $1,200 because he would only be making editorial decisions and having his say in the magazine. What he said in the January 1934 *Crisis* shocked and amazed.

"The thinking colored people of the United States must stop being stampeded by the word segregation."

Du Bois told blacks to embrace voluntary segregation—close ranks with *themselves*.

By then, Du Bois had little hope that he would see an end to prejudice. He no longer felt that racist whites were merely ignorant about black life and history. They were mentally ill, he believed.

Du Bois still decried discrimination but argued that fighting *against* discrimination didn't have to mean fighting *for* integration. Case in point: Jim Crow public school systems. Instead of fighting for school

MARCH, 1933

FIFTEEN CENTS

THE
CRISIS

A RECORD OF THE DARKER RACES

KARL MARX AND THE NEGRO
GREENE · DOERMAN · CASTE · LANGSTON HUGHES

While in Atlanta, Du Bois gave himself a crash course on Karl Marx, often called the "father" of Communism. In "Karl Marx and the Negro," Du Bois spotlighted the contempt Marx had for American slavery.

integration, campaign for black schools to receive the same funding as the white ones, Du Bois reasoned.

Shame on you! howled legions of blacks longing and laboring for integration. They couldn't believe he was pulling a Wizard and a Garvey.

The March *Crisis* carried Walter White's counterpoint. He wanted it known far and wide that the NAACP no way, no how endorsed Du Bois's views.

Du Bois hung tough. To the charge that he had done a crazy about-face, "I am not worried about being inconsistent," he said in the April *Crisis*. "What worries me is the Truth. I am talking about conditions in 1934 and not in 1910. I do not care what I said in 1910 or 1810 or in B.C. 700."

What's more, light-skinned Du Bois accused lighter-skinned White of not being black enough: "Walter White is white. He has more white companions and friends than colored. He goes where he will in New York City and naturally meets no Color Line, for the simple and sufficient reason that he isn't 'colored': he feels his new freedom in bitter contrast to what he was born to in Georgia. This is perfectly natural and he does what anyone else of his complexion would do."

At a mid-May meeting, the NAACP board passed

a resolution forbidding officers from criticizing fellow officers in *The Crisis* without the board's approval.

"I regret to say that I am unable to comply with this vote," Du Bois informed the board in a letter of resignation.

The board didn't accept his resignation. Some hoped for peace between the NAACP and W. E. B.

Du Bois wouldn't take no for an answer. Writing from Atlanta on June 26, 1934, he sent the board a long letter, stating that, no matter what, as of July 1:

> I automatically cease to have any connection whatsoever in any shape or form with the National Association for the Advancement of Colored People. I do not, however, cease to wish it well, to follow it with personal and palpitating interest, and to applaud it when it is able to rescue itself from its present impossible position and reorganize itself according to the demands of the present crisis.
>
> Very respectfully yours,
> W. E. B. Du Bois

THIRTEEN

"WORDS LIKE THESE make effort worthwhile."

June 27, 1934, from Du Bois's reply to Talented Tenther Shirley Graham, then best known for her black-cast opera, *Tom-Toms*. In 1934, this divorcée with two young sons was at work on a master's degree from Oberlin (while family cared for her children).

Back in 1920, when Shirley was thirteen and fifty-something-year-old Du Bois was in Colorado Springs for a speaking engagement, he had stayed in her family's home, where *The Crisis* was required reading.

"For all that you have done for us, we thank you," wrote Shirley Graham in the close of her long, flair-filled letter, written after hearing of Du Bois's first letter of resignation from the NAACP. "We, who are about to live, salute you, our Chief." (He would become a lot more than her "chief.")

In the meantime, Du Bois was chief of AU's sociology department. He had his ducks in a row before he left the NAACP. His job at AU was to be for life, John Hope promised.

The AU that the sixty-six-year-old Du Bois returned to in the 1930s wasn't the same school he left in 1910. With all-male Morehouse and all-female Spelman colleges, it was part of the Atlanta University System. (Morehouse and Spelman offered undergraduate degrees, AU professional and graduate degrees.)

Nothing had changed between Nina and her Will. Though she loathed Atlanta, she had been willing to return there; however, she was no match for her husband's litany of excuses. With Yolande and Baby Du Bois back in Baltimore with Arnett Williams, Nina stayed in New York, living in a smaller apartment in the Dunbar complex, while her husband was a whirlwind: teaching at AU, giving speeches, writing articles, and completing works in progress.

In the summer of 1934, he was wrapping up on a book that refuted the popular take on Reconstruction. *Birth of a Nation* wasn't the only culprit. There were books like the best-selling *The Tragic Era* (1929), which skewered Radical Republicans as power-hungry rogues and black men as brutes and buffoons who never should have been given the vote.

"It seems to me that the *Tragic Era* should be answered—adequately, fully ably, finally," Anna Julia Cooper had written Du Bois, "& again it seems to me that *Thou* art the Man!"

The Man produced a final draft of about seven hundred pages published in June 1935: *Black Reconstruction: An Essay Toward a History of the Part Which Black Folk Played in the Attempt to Reconstruct Democracy in America, 1860–1880.*

Many white reviewers denounced *Black Reconstruction.* More than a few, however, gave this tome its due. Oswald Villard, back again with the NAACP, called it a "remarkable book."

The same month that *Black Reconstruction* came out, Du Bois got a green light on another project. A German-American foundation in Philly, the Oberlaender Trust, was granting him $1,600 to study vocational education in Germany and Austria, to see what vocational schools in the U.S. might learn from them. (Du Bois had more interest in vocational schools now that he embraced voluntary segregation. Black communities would need people as skilled at building libraries as at writing books to fill their shelves.)

"When this is read I shall be sailing on the sea," began Du Bois's piece in a mid-June 1936 issue of the *Pittsburgh Courier*, a major black-owned newspaper in which he now had a column.

As always, Du Bois knew how to make the most of a travel opportunity. His trip began with a week in England, followed by a few days in Belgium. The Germany he entered in July 1936 was Adolf Hitler's Third Reich: a fascist nation, with the government dictating practically all its citizens' actions and attitudes, preaching the supremacy of the Aryan race, and relegating non-Aryans to second-class citizenship, with special venom for Jews.

Berlin put on a somewhat kinder, gentler face as host of that year's summer Olympic Games, in which several black athletes were victors, most of all Jesse Owens, winner of four track-and-field gold medals.

Du Bois had nothing bad to say about Germany in his *Pittsburgh Courier* columns until after he had been to France (which is where he was during most of the Olympics), then to Austria, then back to Germany before leaving that part of Europe for good. Only then did his columns carry his true thoughts on Germany. For one, he called the persecution of Jews "an attack on civilization, comparable only to such horrors as the Spanish Inquisition and the African slave trade."

When Du Bois wrote these words, he had already been back to the USSR, where after a brief stay in Moscow, he boarded the Trans-Siberian Express for a six-thousand-mile journey east to the port city of Vladivostok not far from the Chinese border. Another train took him to Manchukuo, which had been China's Manchuria until Japan seized it (1931) and made it a puppet state. After a week in Manchukuo, Du Bois spent ten days in China, then headed by the anti-communist General Chiang Kai-shek.

Du Bois's adventures in China began in Beijing, with its many wonders, from the Forbidden City to the Great Wall. Then he was on to Nanking, China's capital at the time.

Next city: Shanghai.

Next nation: the Land of the Rising Sun. In Japan, he toured Kyoto, Tokyo, and Nagasaki.

While in the Far East, Du Bois lectured, gave in-terviews, met dignitaries, enjoyed lavish luncheons—was treated like the citizen of the world he considered himself.

His return to the U.S. in late winter 1937 included a stopover in Hawaii—"a night blooming cereus; a riot of color, of flowers." His only regret: that the native peoples were being so exploited by the U.S. corpora-tions that had a lock on Hawaii's sugar and pineapple industries. That aside, Hawaii was a paradise. He told *Pittsburgh Courier* readers, "I think if I lived here, of-ten and of midnight, I would reel down to the sea, and prostrate myself to the awful hills; and cry to the night: who am I that may see and smell and hear this ecstasy . . . this joyous blend of the blood of all races,—I, who belong to a world, so poor, so cruel, so full of hate and hurt."

So angry with the U.S., Du Bois didn't delve into the hate and hurt millions of people endured in the USSR, China, and Japan. For example, Joseph Stalin, the USSR's leader since 1922, was a sociopath, ruling through terror.

A year after his trip around the world, in February 1938, Du Bois recounted his life's journey in the speech, "A Pageant in Seven Decades," in Spelman's Sisters Chapel. The AU system was celebrating his seventieth birthday.

As he had in *Darkwater*, in "A Pageant in Seven Decades" he presented his childhood as more idyllic than it was. This time his father was "dead before I can remember." (He hardly ever mentioned his brother Adelbert in print or conversation.)

Du Bois was clearly proud of his life as he covered his educational conquests and research projects, his founding of periodicals and organizations, and the mountains he climbed along the way. He didn't leave out his travels. Nor how it hurt to leave *The Crisis*— "like giving up a child."

No mention of his son, Burghardt.

No mention of Yolande, whose second marriage had recently ended in divorce.

Once again, all Nina got was a sentence. Along with Yolande and five-year-old Baby Du Bois, Nina was at the fete, after receiving a last-minute invitation.

Near the end of "A Pageant," Du Bois talked about a dream deferred: a multi-volume encyclopedia of the

Standing left to right: presumably a waiter; sociologist Charles S. Johnson, then head of Fisk's social science department; Yolande; James Weldon Johnson; Ira De A. Reid, AU sociology professor; Rufus Clement, John Hope's successor as head of AU; William Stanley Braithwaite, poet and AU English professor. Seated to Du Bois's left, Nina and Joel Spingarn.

black world. He had conceived of it back in 1909, calling it the *Encyclopedia Africana*, but had failed to secure funding for it. Plus, the NAACP came along.

Thirty years later, the project, now named *Encyclopedia of the Negro*, was on the drawing board again, thanks to seed money from the Phelps-Stokes Fund.

"We are seeking a quarter of a million dollars to realize this dream," Du Bois announced in Sisters Chapel.

And he was so grateful to be alive still, to have dreams still. So many of the souls he had known were dead, including T. Thomas Fortune, Clement Morgan, Ida B. Wells, Monroe Trotter, Francis Grimké, and the friend responsible for his being back at AU, John Hope.

What did Du Bois deem the most delicious thing about his life?

That "above all I have done the work which I wanted to do and not merely that which men wished to pay me for." This, he said, is "the essential difference between Heaven and Hell."

In keeping with his heavenly way, Du Bois produced another book on black history, *Black Folk Then and Now* (1939), dedicated to his granddaughter "in the hope that her bright eyes may one day see some of the things I dream."

He had been dreaming of a new scholarly journal, *Phylon* (Greek for race or nation), which premiered in January 1940. Later that year came another book:

Dusk of Dawn, dedicated to Joel Spingarn, who had died in 1939.

"Crucified on the vast wheel of time, I flew round and round with the Zeitgeist, waving my pen and lifting faint voices to explain, expound and exhort; to see, foresee and prophesy, to the few who could or would listen," Du Bois declared early on in *Dusk of Dawn,* part memoir, part analysis of the world: its woes, its wrongs, its wounds. As for black America's future, Du Bois didn't rule anything out: "We may be expelled from the United States as the Jew is being expelled from Germany."

By then, Germany had expelled several hundred thousand souls, most of them Jews, having seized their property and possessions, with worse on the way.

Germany had also invaded Czechoslovakia and Poland, triggering declarations of war from Great Britain and France. Unfazed, Germany moved on to other European nations. Its chief allies were fascist Italy and Japan, which was intent on conquering China and Southeast Asia.

An oil embargo was one of the measures the U.S. took to get Japan to back off. Japan's response: the near obliteration of the U.S. naval forces in Pearl Harbor, Hawaii, on December 7, 1941.

Close to 2,400 dead.

More than 1,000 wounded.

The U.S. promptly declared war on Japan. Germany and Italy then declared war on the U.S., which shot back with a declaration of war on them. The U.S. and its allies now included the USSR, which Germany had attacked.

World War II.

Wounded World II.

Close ranks *again*. That's what Du Bois urged blacks to do in the Harlem-based *Amsterdam News*. "We may sadly admit today that the First World War did not bring us democracy. Nor will the second." But Hitler had to be stopped.

Du Bois was in a war of his own at AU. That celebration of his seventieth birthday had been a must-do because he was a legend, not a sign of a happy family. Du Bois constantly clashed with Florence Read, Spelman's white and very conservative president. She routinely put the kibosh on Spelman students taking his sociology courses. Read had also opposed *Phylon*.

Du Bois's relationship with John Hope's successor as president of AU, Rufus Clement, was equally acidic. Clement had clipped Du Bois's wings by denying him permission to accept an invitation from New York University to teach there for a semester. Back then few predominantly white schools would even think of making such an offer to a black scholar.

Life with Read and Clement only got worse. Two days before Thanksgiving 1943, he received a letter, which began:

"Dear Doctor Du Bois:

Pursuant to the action of the Board of Trustees of Atlanta University . . ."

FOURTEEN

"WITHOUT A WORD of warning I found myself at the age of 76 without employment and with less than $5,000 of savings."

AU got rid of Du Bois on a technicality: mandatory retirement at age sixty-five. (When he returned to AU full-time back in 1934, he was already sixty-six.)

His retirement was to be effective June 30, 1944. The pushout came with a year's salary ($4,500). A pension of $1,800 would kick in after 1945.

Du Bois was not unemployed for long. The NAACP invited him back. It was an act of grace, spearheaded by two friends: Arthur Spingarn, by then the NAACP's president, and Dr. Louis Wright, its first black chairman of the board and Du Bois's physician.

Circa 1940s. His hands look as they do because of vitiligo, a disease that causes skin to lose pigment.

Du Bois's salary: $5,000 a year. His title: Director of Special Research. Mandatory retirement age: None. He could only be fired if he ceased to be of value.

When Du Bois returned to New York City, he moved into an apartment in Harlem, at 409 Edgecombe Avenue. The apartment hunting had been handled by Shirley Graham. The two had reconnected in 1936, two years after her "We who are about to live, salute you, our Chief" letter. Mutual admiration moved up to romance. (Du Bois and Jessie Fauset had been history a long time ago. Between Jessie and Shirley, he had numerous affairs, sometimes juggling more than one at a time.)

Nina was no longer in New York. Along with Yolande and her daughter, she was back in Baltimore, living in a house Papa Du Bois had built for them.

Many people thought Du Bois would be no more than an NAACP knickknack.

Think again.

Between 1944 and 1948—"I attended the Fifth Pan-African Congress in England, wrote two books on colonies and Africa, edited two others and wrote many articles, pamphlets and newspaper columns. I attended several conferences and traveled 20,000 miles to deliver 150 lectures on subjects connected with my work for the NAACP as I conceived it."

And during those four years, what a wounded world.

More than 60 million people had died in World War II, which had ended in 1945, after the U.S. dropped atomic bombs on the Japanese cities of Hiroshima and Nagasaki, incinerating about 100,000 people and subjecting tens of thousands to severe burns and radiation poisoning.

Sensitive souls were reeling from the horrors of Hitler's regime: the gas chambers, the mass graves, the emaciated concentration-camp survivors. Over 11 million people slaughtered because evil had been allowed to grow. More than half of the murdered children and adults were Jews. Romany, Poles, Slavs, disabled people, gays, and others branded undesirable, defective—inferior—made up the other millions gone.

Blacks who had served in the U.S. military overseas came home to a nation that was still a shameful land: still lynching, disfranchising, encouraging ignorance, stealing from and insulting blacks.

For people of color around the world, the developments in India were a source of hope. In 1947, after Mahatma Gandhi's years-long nonviolent campaign, India's independence from Great Britain finally occurred. That inspired other colonized people to start or step up freedom campaigns. African liberation leaders included Kwame Nkrumah from Great Britain's Gold Coast. Born in 1909 (like the NAACP), Nkrumah had been speaking out against imperialism since his youth, including when he was a student in the U.S. (at Lincoln University and the University of Pennsylvania).

Nkrumah moved to Manchester, England, in 1945, where he co-organized the Fifth Pan-African Congress held there in mid-October 1945. Du Bois was the guiding spirit. Young firebrands looked upon him as he had regarded Alexander Crummell, hailing Du Bois as the "Father" of Pan-Africanism. The reverence was a much-needed lift, for Du Bois was bearing a personal burden.

Shortly before he set out for England, Nina, like his mother, had a stroke, which left her paralyzed on her left side. It happened while she was in New York for the summer, staying at the Harlem YWCA because her Will wouldn't let her stay in his apartment. "I can quite understand that you do not care for company," she had written, promising not to be a bother, only asking, *Wasn't there a couch on which she could sleep?* This was several weeks after she suffered a bad fall in Baltimore.

When Nina had a stroke, her Will got her into one of New York City's best hospitals, then headed for the Pan-African Congress. Months later, when Nina was well enough to travel, she would return to Baltimore. Her Will would pay for her to have in-home care and would occasionally visit the home in which Yolande and her daughter also still lived.

Why not slow down, ease up? Arthur Spingarn and Louis Wright had asked Papa Du Bois. Perhaps only Shirley Graham could fully appreciate that, though Du Bois was pushing eighty, work was still his heavenly way. (By 1945, Graham had written and produced several plays and the first of her many books for young folks.)

There was nothing heavenly about Du Bois's situation at the NAACP. For one, he was given a small office after having asked for a space large enough to comfortably accommodate himself, his secretary, his many file cabinets, and 2,500 books.

Du Bois's little office shared a wall with that of Thurgood Marshall, the brilliant and raucous head of the NAACP Legal and Educational Defense Fund, which was challenging Jim Crow in the courts.

Hooked on *The Crisis* since he was a teenager, Thurgood Marshall was in awe of Du Bois, who apparently arranged his office to dissuade visitors. "His whole office was fenced in with books that ran all around the room," Marshall recalled, and he never forgot the day he tried to break the ice.

"Look, Doc, your office and mine are side by side and you come in here every morning and you just walk right by."

As Du Bois entered his office, he said, "Yeah, that's one of my bad habits," then shut the door.

NAACP chief Walter White's main problem with Du Bois wasn't that he was aloof but that he was a loose canon—still promoting voluntary segregation and still very critical of Walter White's leadership. Plus, Du Bois was still praising the USSR and increasingly associating with communists, whose ranks included his girlfriend Shirley Graham.

In early September 1948, the NAACP decided that Du Bois had ceased to be of value.

Du Bois neither gave up nor shut up. He accepted an offer from actor-singer-activist Paul Robeson to serve as vice-chair of the Council on African Affairs (CAA). Robeson, who cheered the USSR and criticized the U.S. on several counts—racial injustice among them—had cofounded the CAA in the late 1930s to keep Americans up on current events in Africa. The CAA could not give Du Bois a salary, but he had office space in its Manhattan headquarters and use of its secretary.

The CAA was among many groups on the U.S. Attorney General's list of subversive organizations. Another Red Scare was dawning.

Tensions between the U.S. and the USSR over postwar spheres of influence had led to a Cold War. The USSR was pledged to the spread of communism, the U.S. to stopping that. The Cold War had millions in the U.S. and elsewhere fearing World War III and therefore promoting peace. Once again, Du Bois was in the forefront.

Late March 1949: Along with Paul Robeson, and the white American playwrights Lillian Hellman and Arthur Miller, Du Bois was among the nearly three thousand scholars, scientists, and artists at a peace conference held at New York City's Waldorf-Astoria.

"Why don't you go back to Russia, you stinking Commies?" was one invective hurled by people picketing the conference.

"This conference was not called to defend communism nor socialism nor the American way of life," said Du Bois at a rally in Madison Square Garden on the conference's final day. "It was called to promote peace! It was called to say and say again that no matter how right or wrong differing systems of beliefs in religion, industry or government may be, war is not the method by which their differences can successfully be settled for the good of mankind."

Late April 1949: Along with Robeson, Shirley Graham, Spanish artist Pablo Picasso, and about two thousand promoters of peace, Du Bois was in Paris for the founding of the Communist-led World Peace Council.

August 1949: He was at a peace conference in Moscow.

By then, war had been declared on Paul Robeson. U.S. authorities, long wanting to silence him, seized upon an occassion to condemn him as un-American and turn the public against him. The pivotal moment came when the Associated Press (AP) put out a false report on Robeson's remarks at the Paris peace conference. For starters, the AP claimed that Robeson had compared the U.S. government to Nazi Germany. Branded a traitor, Robeson soon found his career pretty much over in the U.S. What's more, many Talented Tenthers shunned him—but not Du Bois, who continued to have his say.

In April 1950, Du Bois cofounded Peace Information Center (PIC) to keep Americans informed on matters of war and peace. His core comrades included Abbott Simon, a World War II vet, who had seen what the atomic bomb did to Hiroshima.

At the top of PIC's agenda was getting people to sign a petition to ban atomic weapons so that what happened to Hiroshima and Nagasaki would never happen again. The petition was called the Stockholm Appeal because it came out of a March 1950 World Peace Council conference in Stockholm, Sweden. Many, many millions worldwide would sign the Stockholm Appeal, from little-known peace activists to well-known figures such as the Irish writer George Bernard Shaw. In some cases, the signer was a government body—the USSR's parliament, for one.

World War III seemed imminent in late June 1950. USSR-backed North Korea invaded U.S.-backed South Korea. Would President Truman unleash the atomic bomb on North Korea? (The Korean War would end in 1953 without another use of the atomic bomb, but when the war broke out no one had a crystal ball.)

On July 12, 1950, the U.S. Secretary of State, Dean Acheson, publicly skewered the Stockholm Appeal as "a propaganda trick" of the USSR. People who supported the appeal were un-American, he implied.

Du Bois sounded back in a press release: "Does it not occur to you, Sir, that there are honest Americans who, regardless of their differences on other questions, hate and fear war and are determined to do something to avert it?" Du Bois also denounced the Red Scare: "Today in this country it is becoming standard reaction to call anything 'communist' and therefore subversive and unpatriotic, which anybody for any reason dislikes." This tactic, he added, "has already gone too far."

On July 15, the *Chicago Globe* carried a piece by Du Bois on a different subject, in a different tone: "I Bury My Wife."

Nina had died on July 1 and been buried in Great Barrington beside Burghardt "in the sunshine and under the great and beautiful elms." In this remembrance of his wife of more than fifty years, Du Bois described Nina as she was when they first met, "with her great mass of coiled black hair and extraordinarily beautiful eyes." More important, he wanted people to know that Nina had been a loyal, dutiful wife. As for himself: "I was not, on the whole, what one would describe as a good husband. The family and its interests were never the main center of my life. I was always striving to guide the world and certainly the Negro group."

No plans to stop.

August 1950: He was in Prague to speak at the World Youth Conference.

September–October 1950: He was on the campaign trail as the American Labor Party's candidate for a U.S. Senate seat. He didn't expect to win; he only hoped to guide the world.

"Du Bois Tells Harlem Only U.S. Wants War" was the *New York Times* headline for its October 6, 1950, report on a speech in which the eighty-two-year-old candidate upbraided the U.S., which "forces other nations to fight, and asks you and me to impoverish ourselves, give up health and schools, sacrifice our sons to a jim-crow army, and commit suicide for a world war that nobody wants but the rich Americans who profit by it." He urged the 1,500-person crowd at Harlem's Golden Gate Ballroom to repudiate U.S. military and political bigwigs who boast "'we can lick the world.'"

Time to lick Du Bois, some said.

FIFTEEN

"IT IS A CURIOUS THING that today I am called upon to defend myself against criminal charges for openly advocating the one thing all people want—peace."

February 16, 1951, in D.C.: Du Bois and four PIC colleagues had been arraigned, then released on bail.

Back in 1950, after Du Bois rebuked Dean Acheson, PIC heard from the Department of Justice (DOJ). It demanded that PIC register as a foreign agent of the USSR. The USSR was not PIC's handler. Du Bois was no one's agent but his own. Rather than go to war with the DOJ, PIC disbanded in October 1950.

Not good enough. The DOJ still insisted that PIC register as a foreign agent even though it no longer existed. When the DOJ didn't get satisfaction, indictments were handed down in early February 1951.

Du Bois and Shirley Graham had planned to marry at the end of the month. After the indictment, they moved up the date, to February 14, two days before the PIC Five surrendered to the authorities in D.C. and nine days before W. E. B. turned eighty-three.

A birthday party had long been planned, to be held at Essex House in midtown Manhattan. Within days of Du Bois's indictment, the hotel notified the head of the birthday party committee, sociologist E. Franklin Frazier, that it could no longer honor the reservation. What's more, waves of people who had RSVP'd yes canceled, many Talented Tenthers among them.

Frazier secured another venue, Smalls Paradise in Harlem. Du Bois was deeply grateful to those who showed up, but still soul-sick about those who had cut him loose. The faithful included Paul Robeson. He would stand by Du Bois in the months leading up to the trial, set for November. Part of Du Bois couldn't wait. He was eager for his day in court, eager to put the *U.S. government* on trial for political persecution. He never got the chance.

"DU BOIS, 4 OTHERS ACQUITTED, JUDGE REJECTS GOV'T FRAMEUP," cheered the November 21, 1951, issue of the *Daily Worker*, a newspaper of the Communist Party USA (CPUSA). The prosecution had no case. It had all been an intent to intimidate.

Though he was vindicated, Du Bois's life became harder. Few periodicals wanted to carry his articles. Book publishers rejected his manuscripts. Requests for speaking engagements dwindled. He would find himself forced to sell his grandparents' homeplace.

Du Bois's ability to travel outside the continental U.S. was curtailed, because the State Department had voided his and his wife's passports. (The passports of Paul Robeson and other left-wing activists had also been revoked.)

To get his passport Du Bois would have to comply with the State Department's request that he state whether he was a Communist.

Never. Du Bois refused to go along with what he saw as an invasion of privacy.

Standing his ground meant passing on several invitations from abroad. One was the March 1957 ceremonies surrounding the Gold Coast becoming the independent nation of Ghana, with Kwame Nkrumah its prime minister. What a wonder that would have been for Du Bois to witness.

Du Bois continued to speak his mind in the few forums still available to him, mostly left-wing newspapers and magazines, such as *The Daily Worker* and *Masses and Mainstream*. The founder of this last periodical was Herbert Aptheker, a CPUSA member with whom Du Bois had become good friends. Aptheker would also publish his books, starting with *In Battle for Peace,* about the trial and acquittal of the PIC Five, which came out in 1952.

A year later, another radical, Howard Fast, published the fiftieth-anniversary edition of *The Souls of Black Folk* through his small press, Blue Heron. In addition to tweaking some of the pieces, Du Bois added a new introduction. In it, he revised a famous declaration.

> I still think today as yesterday that the color line is a great problem of this century. But today I see more clearly than yesterday that back of the problem of race and color, lies a greater problem which both obscures and implements

it: and that is the fact that so many civilized persons are willing to live in comfort even if the price of this is poverty, ignorance and disease of the majority of their fellowmen; that to maintain this privilege men have waged war until today war tends to become universal and continuous.

Du Bois also had fiction in the hopper, resulting in the Black Flame trilogy, which Aptheker would publish. The three novels—*The Ordeal of Mansart* (1957), *Mansart Builds a School* (1959), and *Worlds of Color* (1961)—are a saga of the family of Southern-born educator Manuel Mansart that begins in 1876 and ends in 1954.

May 17, 1954. "I have seen the impossible happen," Du Bois wrote of this day on which the U.S. Supreme Court declared segregated public schools unconstitutional in its *Brown v. Board of Education* decision—the NAACP's greatest victory, with future U.S. Supreme Court Justice Thurgood Marshall the lead lawyer on the case. Many people saw the *Brown* decision as the beginning of the end of Jim Crow.

A year after *Brown* came the Montgomery Bus Boycott, led by Martin Luther King Jr. With degrees from Morehouse, Crozer Seminary, and Boston University, King was a Talented Tenther of whom Du Bois could be proud. Du Bois had long since despaired that so many of black America's best and brightest were more concerned with comfortable lives than with lives of service.

Not King. And while Du Bois admired the movement King led, he feared that any day "their leader will be killed."

Du Bois got a new lease on life in spring 1958, when the U.S. Supreme Court ruled that it was unconstitutional to deny people passports because of their politics or refusal to state them. A few months later, in August, after more than 2,500 days of feeling like prisoners in the land of their birth, the Du Boises embarked on a great excursion into the world.

Highlights in Europe included his receiving an honorary degree from Humboldt University, the University of Berlin's new name. The Du Boises rang in the New Year in Moscow, at a party in the Kremlin. After several months in the USSR, they headed to the

Having a laugh with China's chief Mao Zedong.

People's Republic of China, as mainland China, now Communist, called itself.

The Du Boises returned home a few days before the Fourth of July 1959—then traveled some more.

July 1960: They were in Ghana for some nation-

O, Happy Day!—with wife Shirley at a reception following the inauguration of Nkrumah (far left).

al festivities. Kwame Nkrumah was now president. While in Ghana, Du Bois spoke with Nkrumah about that fifty-year-old dream of an encyclopedia of the black world. The Phelps-Stokes Fund had long ago abandoned the *Encyclopedia of the Negro*. Du Bois was back to calling it the *Encyclopedia Africana*.

November 1960: Back to Africa. This time to Nigeria as guests of Nnamdi Azikiwe, the newly elected Governor-General of this now independent nation. Du Bois had made the journey even though he suffered a minor stroke during a layover in London.

Stop overworking?

Back in the U.S., the Du Boises were aboard a new magazine, *Freedomways.* Cofounders included playwright Lorraine Hansberry, best known for her play *A Raisin in the Sun.*

A huge world of work opened up to Du Bois when he received a cable from Kwame Nkrumah in February 1961. The *Encyclopedia Africana* was a go!

Within weeks of that good news, Du Bois experienced a parent's worst nightmare. Again.

On March 21, Yolande died of a heart attack.

As he had done with her mother and the brother she never knew, ninety-three-year-old Lovingly Papa buried his sixty-year-old daughter in Great Barrington.

"Why?" he asked Shirley, shortly after he learned of his daughter's death. "I am old; Yolande had so much life before her. Why should she go and I remain?"

Was life still worth the striving?

SIXTEEN

"TO GUS HALL:

"On this first day of October, 1961, I am applying for admission to membership in the Communist Party of the United States. I have been long and slow in coming to this conclusion, but at last my mind is settled. . . .

"Capitalism cannot reform itself; it is doomed to self-destruction. No universal selfishness can bring social good to all.

"Communism—the effort to give all men what they need and to ask of each the best they can contribute—this is the only way of human life."

Shortly after Du Bois wrote this letter to the head of the CPUSA, he and his wife were off to Ghana.

Home was atop a hill in the capital, Accra, courtesy of the Ghanian government. The Du Boises' seven-room bungalow was a mecca for hungry minds living in or visiting Ghana. There were luncheons, dinners, and sometimes just talk time on the verandah.

When Du Bois didn't have company *or* wasn't giving a lecture *or* an interview to a journalist *or* taking a nap *or* a walk in the hills of Accra, he was working on the *Encyclopedia Africana or* putting the final touches on another autobiography *or* writing short pieces.

There came a day when he couldn't do much work. Frail but not totally befogged, he kept up with current events, like the March on Washington for Jobs and Freedom, set for August 28, 1963.

On that day, a multiracial quarter-million crowd gathered at the Washington Mall, where Martin Luther King Jr. would speak of his great dream.

But before that moment, there was an announcement from Roy Wilkins, by then NAACP chief. The night before, around midnight, ninety-five-year-old W. E. B. Du Bois had passed.

"Regardless of the fact that in his later years, Dr. Du Bois chose another path," Wilkins told the still, solemn crowd, "it is incontrovertible that at the dawn of the twentieth century his was the voice calling you to gather here today in this cause."

William Edward Burghardt Du Bois never raised a visible empire in Africa, but he did make a name for himself in social science and in literature. Without a doubt, he did his utmost to uplift his race, convinced that when people regarded as the least are raised, the whole world gains. And so, for seventy years, Du Bois had given voice to black strivings.

Teaching.

Speech-making.

Cofounding and furthering organizations, from the American Negro Academy through the Niagara Movement, the NAACP, and PIC.

Fathering periodicals—*The Moon*, *The Horizon*, *The Crisis*, *Phylon*, *Freedomways*.

Producing pamphlets, bulletins, and studies.

Writing more than twenty books, thousands of articles, and scores of creative pieces.

And traveling the world.

Roy Wilkins called for a moment of silence.

It was a cheer for a weary traveler.

February 23, 1963—his ninety-fifth birthday. He had just received an honorary degree from the University of Ghana.

SOURCE NOTES

EPIGRAPH

"The pronunciation of . . .": Lewis, *W.E.B. Du Bois: Biography*, 11.

INTRODUCTION

"O I wonder . . .": Aptheker, *Against Racism*, 28.

"great bitterness . . . great ambition": Aptheker, *Against Racism*, 17.

"by telling the wonderful . . .": Du Bois, "Strivings of the Negro People," 194.

CHAPTER ONE

"Dear Mam . . .": Aptheker, *Correspondence,* vol. 1, 3.

"first great excursion . . .": Du Bois, *Autobiography*, 62.

"The grounds . . . name is there": Aptheker, *Correspondence,* vol. 1, 3.

"Do bana coba . . .": Du Bois, *Dusk*, 58.

"The railroad runs . . . I was there": Aptheker, *Correspondence*, vol. 1, 4.

"of every hue . . ." and "the swaggering men . . .": Du Bois, *Autobiography*, 63.

CHAPTER TWO

"During my trip": Aptheker, *Newspaper Columns*, vol. 1, 6.

"fierce brave voice": Aptheker, *Selections from "The Horizon,"* 16.

"Pleased to see . . . to be neglected": Aptheker, *Newspaper Columns*, vol. 1, 6.

"Ought the Indian . . .": Aptheker, *Newspaper Columns*, vol. 1, 5.

"Should Indians be . . ." Aptheker, *Newspaper Columns*, vol. 1, 6.

"I did not . . .": Aptheker, *Newspaper Columns*, vol. 1, 1.

"The colored people . . .": Aptheker, *Newspaper Columns*, vol. 1, 3.

"Though we have . . . within their power": *National Convention of Colored Men*, 5.

"young Willie Du Bois . . .": Aptheker, *Annotated Bibliography*, 3.

"repeated applause": Lewis, *W.E.B. Du Bois: Biography*, 50.

"solemn feel of wings!": Du Bois, *Autobiography*, 65.

CHAPTER THREE

"Our University is . . . New England hills": Aptheker, *Correspondence*, vol. 1, 5.

"Oh, she was . . .": Aptheker, *Creative Writings*, 56.

"Lynching was a . . . upon my soul": Du Bois, *Autobiography*, 77.

"For those who . . .": Du Bois, *Fisk Herald*, October 1886, 7.

"Why isn't there . . .": Aptheker, *Annotated Bibliography*, 7.

"the power and purpose . . . if he will": Lewis, *W.E.B. Du Bois: Biography*, 77.

"Willie is no more.": Lewis, *W.E.B. Du Bois: Biography*, 79.

"Age of Miracles": Du Bois, *Darkwater*, 7.

"I sought no . . .": Sollors et al., *Blacks at Harvard*, 74.

"to enlarge my grasp . . .": Sollors et al., *Blacks at Harvard*, 72.

"Words and ideas . . .": Du Bois, *Autobiography*, 90.

"I believe, foolishly . . .": Aptheker, *Against Racism*, 17.

"the advance of a part . . .": Aptheker, *Against Racism*, 14.

"if they have . . .": Sollors et al., *Blacks at Harvard*, 84.

"must not herd . . .": Huggins, *W.E.B. Du Bois: Writings*, 1249.

"If there is any . . .": Aptheker, *Correspondence*, vol. 1, 10.

"I am a Negro . . .": Aptheker, *Correspondence*, vol. 1, 11.

"I think you . . .": Aptheker, *Correspondence*, vol. 1, 14.

"You expressed the hope . . .": Aptheker, *Correspondence*, vol. 1, 16.

"to support him . . .": Aptheker, *Correspondence*, vol. 1, 17.

"including beer and tip": Aptheker, *Against Racism*, 32.

"If more economically . . .": Aptheker, *Against Racism*, 33.

"I did not . . .": Sollors et al., *Blacks at Harvard*, 81.

"a wander": Aptheker, *Against Racism*, 27.

"A Fellow of Harvard": Lewis, *W.E.B. Du Bois: Biography*, 154.

"a curious little ceremony": Du Bois, *Autobiography*, 107.

"Sacrifice to the Zeitgeist": Aptheker, *Against Racism*, 27.

"as a strong man . . . very reason incomprehensible": Aptheker, *Against Racism*, 27–28.

"If by being . . . do not object": Aptheker, *Correspondence*, vol. 3, 223.

"striving to make . . .": Aptheker, *Against Racism*, 28.

"work for the rise . . . France or Germany": Aptheker, *Against Racism*, 29.

"'nigger'-hating America!": Du Bois, *Darkwater*, 8.

CHAPTER FOUR

"President Washington Sir!" and "Your wife knows . . .": Aptheker, *Correspondence*, vol. 1, 37.

"Can give mathematics . . .": Aptheker, *Correspondence*, vol. 1, 38.

"a few piles . . .": Du Bois, *Autobiography*, 119.

"Professor Du Bois will . . ." and "No, he won't": Du Bois, *Autobiography*, 117.

"some absorbing moral . . .": Moses, *Alexander Crummell*, 246.

"In all things . . .": ASALH, *The Niagara Movement*, 15.

"Agitation . . . the extremest folly": ASALH, *The Niagara Movement*, 16.

"The speech stamps . . .": Harlan, *Booker T. Washington*, 222.

"a word fitly spoken": Aptheker, *Correspondence*, vol. 1, 39.

"If you hear . . .": Harlan, *Booker T. Washington Papers*, vol. 4, 99.

"Are ready to . . .": Aptheker, *Correspondence*, vol. 1, 40.

"going to the dogs": Du Bois, *Dusk*, 30.

"The Negro problem . . .": Du Bois, *Autobiography*, 124.

"through carelessness and moral . . . ought to be done.": Du Bois, *Suppression*, 37.

"a valuable review . . .": Du Bois, *Suppression*, xxv.

"typical families . . . to get aid": Du Bois, *Philadelphia Negro*, 197–98.

"We don't work . . .": Du Bois, *Philadelphia Negro*, 233.

"where kids played . . ." and "I sat down . . .": Du Bois, *Autobiography*, 123.

CHAPTER FIVE

"Strivings of the Negro People": Du Bois, *Atlantic Monthly*, August 1897, 194–98.

"The hundred hills . . . against the sky": Du Bois, *Autobiography*, 134.

"he pulled on your . . .": Lewis, *W.E.B. Du Bois: Biography*, 217.

"I did not . . .": Du Bois, *Autobiography*, 141.

"We seemed to . . . 'Niggers!'" Du Bois, *Souls*, 1903 edition, 101.

"To the Nations of the World": Lewis, *W.E.B. Du Bois: A Reader*, 639–41.

"gospel of Work . . . terms with whites": Du Bois, "The Evolution of Negro Leadership."

"For every right . . .": Sollors et al., *Blacks at Harvard*, 91.

CHAPTER SIX

"HEREIN lie buried . . .": Du Bois, *Souls*, 1903 edition, 1.

"Instinctively I bowed . . .": Du Bois, *Souls*, 1903 edition, 103.

"never faltered, he . . .": Du Bois, *Souls*, 1903 edition, 108.

"the fear of . . .": Du Bois, *Souls*, 1903 edition, 99.

"wasting, wasting away": Du Bois, *Souls*, 1903 edition, 100.

"He died at . . .": Du Bois, *Souls*, 1903 edition, 101.

"To Burghardt and Yolande . . .": Du Bois, *Souls*, 1903 edition, front matter.

"Atlanta Compromise": Du Bois, *Souls*, 1903 edition, 22.

"the disfranchisement of the Negro . . .": Du Bois, *Souls*, 1903 edition, 26.

"we must unceasingly . . .": Du Bois, *Souls*, 1903 edition, 29.

"of death and suffering . . .": Du Bois, *Souls*, 1903 edition, 123.

"Let us cheer . . .": Du Bois, *Souls*, 1903 edition, 128–29.

"THE SOULS OF BLACK . . .": Aptheker, *Literary Legacy*, 53.

"an aching sense . . .": *The Nation*, June 11, 1903, 481.

"vigor, spontaneity, and spirituality": Aptheker, *Literary Legacy*, 53.

"that Mr. Washington's . . . entire race": Duster, *Crusade for Justice*, 280–81.

"worthy to be classed . . .": Aptheker, *Correspondence*, vol. 1, 60.

"Professor Du Bois . . . book, didn't it?": Aptheker, *Correspondence*, vol. 1, 66.

"Benedict Arnold of the Negro race": Fox, *The Guardian*, 9.

"Are the rope . . .": Fox, *The Guardian*, 51.

"unselfishness, pureness of heart . . . leading the way backward": Aptheker, *Correspondence*, vol. 1, 68.

"unceasingly, and if . . .": Aptheker, *Writings by W.E.B. Du Bois*, vol. 1, 202.

CHAPTER SEVEN

"Credo": Aptheker, *Writings by W.E.B. Du Bois,* vol. 1, 229–30.

"a very dangerous": Aptheker, *Correspondence*, vol. 1, 103.

"Agitation . . . of all races": Aptheker, *Pamphlets*, 58.

"Address to the Country": Aptheker, *Pamphlets*, 63–65.

CHAPTER EIGHT

"A Litany of Atlanta": Aptheker, *Creative Writings*, 7–9.

"Kill the niggers": Crowe, "Racial Massacre in Atlanta," 155.

"If a white mob . . .": Du Bois, *Autobiography*, 181.

"amazed & disgusted . . ." and "there are really . . .": Aptheker, *Correspondence*, vol. 1, 123.

"failure existed as . . .": Aptheker, *Selections from "The Horizon,"* vii.

"If the truth . . .": Aptheker, *Selections from "The Horizon,"* 3.

"Socialist-of-the . . . Get and Grab": Aptheker, *Selections from "The Horizon,"* 6.

"Buy books . . . Buy books": Aptheker, *Selections from "The Horizon,"* 13.

"kept up the campaign . . .": Aptheker, *Selections from "The Horizon,"* 27.

"Dear Sir: . . .": Aptheker, *Selections from "The Horizon,"* 32.

"An Essay by . . .": Aptheker, *Selections from "The Horizon,"* 37.

"The Niagara Movement . . . shoot to kill": Aptheker, *Selections from "The Horizon,"* 69–70.

"Curse the day . . .": Lewis, *W.E.B. Du Bois: Biography*, 388.

"Was I doing . . ." and "Who realizes the seriousness": Ovington, *Black and White Sat Down Together*, 55.

"a visible bursting . . .": Aptheker, *Writings by W.E.B. Du Bois*, vol. 1, 399.

CHAPTER NINE

"The object of this . . .": Huggins, *W.E.B. Du Bois: Writings*, 1131.

"Once to every . . .": bartleby.com

"Save us, World-Spirit . . .": Aptheker, *Creative Writings*, 23.

"mass of gray . . . wettest of rains": Huggins, *W.E.B. Du Bois: Writings*, 1167.

"most distinguished": Lewis, *W.E.B. Du Bois: Biography*, 501.

"either as an ignorant . . .": Lewis, *W.E.B. Du Bois: Biography*, 507.

"I do not . . .": Aptheker, *Correspondence*, vol. 1, 203.

CHAPTER TEN

"Above all remember . . .": Aptheker, *Correspondence*, vol. 1, 208.

"very slovenly": Lewis, *W.E.B. Du Bois: Biography*, 452.

"the ability to . . . discipline": Aptheker, *Correspondence*, vol. 1, 208.

"I can't help . . .": Lewis, *W.E.B. Du Bois: Biography*, 465.

"Ouchie": Lewis, *W.E.B. Du Bois: Biography*, 454.

"Your illness has made . . ." and "I am glad . . .": Aptheker, *Correspondence*, vol. 1, 221.

"Mr. President, why . . .": Franklin, *From Slavery*, 308.

"President of all . . .": Lewis, *W.E.B. Du Bois: Biography*, 423.

"justice done to . . .": Franklin, *From Slavery*, 292.

"Let us not . . .": Lewis, *W.E.B. Du Bois: A Reader*, 697.

"spread of European . . . is not ashamed": Huggins, *W.E.B. Du Bois: Writings*, 1179.

CHAPTER ELEVEN

"Returning Soldiers": Huggins, *W.E.B. Du Bois: Writings*, 1179–81.

"Like men we'll . . .": Franklin, *From Slavery*, 316.

"The haters of black . . .": Lewis, *W.E.B. Du Bois: The Fight*, 24.

"a slip of a girl . . .": Du Bois, *Darkwater*, 9.

"very serious defects . . . for real organization": Huggins, *W.E.B. Du Bois: Writings*, 971.

"It was not . . ." and "He only appreciates . . .": Vincent, *Voices*, 97.

"little, fat, black . . ." and "Now, what does . . .": Vincent, *Voices*, 99.

"a monstrosity": Vincent, *Voices*, 100.

"the most dangerous enemy . . .": Huggins, *W.E.B. Du Bois: Writings*, 990.

"I do not . . .": Aptheker, *Selections from "The Crisis,"* 448.

CHAPTER TWELVE

"when shall I forget . . .": Du Bois, *Dusk*, 59.

"the Spirit longs . . .": Aptheker, *Creative Writings*, 131.

"Yet, there lay an . . .": Du Bois, *Dusk*, 143.

"Why should there . . . So the Girl Marries": Du Bois, *The Crisis*, June 1928, 209.

"The thinking colored . . .": Du Bois, *The Crisis*, January 1934, 20.

"I am not worried . . ." and "Walter White is white . . .": Aptheker, *Selections from "The Crisis,"* 745.

"I regret to say . . .": Aptheker, *Correspondence*, vol. 1, 478.

"I automatically cease . . .": Aptheker, *Correspondence*, vol. 1, 480–81.

CHAPTER THIRTEEN

"Words like these . . ." and "For all that . . . you, our Chief":
  Aptheker, *Correspondence*, vol. 1, 484.

"It seems to . . . art the Man!": Aptheker, *Correspondence*, vol. 1,
  411.

"remarkable book": Du Bois, *Black Reconstruction*, xxxi.

"When this is read . . .": Aptheker, *Newspaper Columns*, vol. 1, 81.

"an attack on civilization . . .": Aptheker, *Newspaper Columns*,
  vol. 1, 149.

"a night blooming cereus . . .": Aptheker, *Newspaper Columns*,
  vol. 1, 184.

"I think if . . . hate and hurt": Aptheker, *Newspaper Columns*,
  vol. 1, 185.

"dead before I . . .": Aptheker, *Pamphlets*, 244.

"like giving up . . .": Aptheker, *Pamphlets*, 271.

"We are seeking . . .": Aptheker, *Pamphlets*, 272.

"above all I . . . Heaven and Hell": Aptheker, *Pamphlets*, 273.

"in the hope that . . .": Du Bois, *Black Folk*, front matter.

"Crucified on the vast . . .": Du Bois, *Dusk*, 1.

"We may be . . .": Du Bois, *Dusk*, 152.

"We may sadly . . .": Aptheker, *Newspaper Columns*, vol. 1, 414.

"Dear Doctor Du Bois . . .": Aptheker, *Correspondence*, vol. 2, 390.

CHAPTER FOURTEEN

"Without a word . . .": Du Bois, *Autobiography*, 207.

"I attended the Fifth . . .": Du Bois, *Autobiography*, 211–12.

"I can quite . . .": Lewis, *W.E.B. Du Bois: The Fight*, p. 513.

"His whole office . . ." "Look, Doc, your . . ." and "Yeah, that's one . . .": Williams, *Thurgood Marshall*, 167.

"Why don't you . . .": *Time* magazine, "Tumult at the Waldorf," April 4, 1949.

"This conference was . . . the good of mankind": Du Bois, *In Battle*, 17.

"a propaganda trick": *New York Times*, July 13, 1950, 7.

"Does it not . . . gone too far": Du Bois, *In Battle*, 24–25.

"I Bury My Wife": Lewis, *W.E.B. Du Bois: A Reader*, 142–43.

"Du Bois Tells . . . lick the world": *New York Times*, October 6, 1950, 21.

CHAPTER FIFTEEN

"It is a curious . . .": Lewis, *W.E.B. Du Bois: The Fight*, 549.

"DU BOIS, 4 OTHERS . . .": Lewis, *W.E.B. Du Bois: The Fight*, 683.

"I still think . . .": Du Bois, *Souls*, 1953 edition, xi.

"I have seen . . .": Aptheker, *Newspaper Columns*, vol. 2, 931.

"their leader will . . .": Aptheker, *Newspaper Columns*, vol. 2, 983.

"Why? . . . and I remain?": Graham Du Bois, *His Day*, 317.

CHAPTER SIXTEEN

"To Gus Hall . . . of human life": Aptheker, *Correspondence*, vol. 3, 439.

"Regardless of the fact . . . in this cause": Lewis, *W.E.B. Du Bois: Biography*, 2.

BIBLIOGRAPHY

Aptheker, Herbert, editor. *Against Racism: Unpublished Essays, Papers, Addresses, 1887–1961, by W.E.B. Du Bois.* Amherst: University of Massachusetts Press, 1985.

———. *Annotated Bibliography of the Published Writings of W.E.B. Du Bois.* Millwood, N.Y.: Kraus-Thomson, 1973.

———. *The Correspondence of W.E.B. Du Bois,* vols. 1–3. Amherst: University of Massachusetts Press, 1997.

———. *Creative Writings by W.E.B. Du Bois: A Pageant, Poems, Short Stories, and Playlets.* White Plains, N.Y.: Kraus-Thomson, 1985.

———. *The Literary Legacy of W.E.B. Du Bois.* White Plains, N.Y.: Kraus International Publications, 1989.

———. *Newspaper Columns by W.E.B. Du Bois,* vols. 1–2. White Plains, N.Y.: Kraus-Thomson, 1986.

———. *Pamphlets and Leaflets by W.E.B. Du Bois.* White Plains, N.Y.: Kraus-Thomson, 1986.

—————. *Writings by W.E.B. Du Bois in Periodicals Edited by Others*, vols. 1–4. Millwood, N.Y.: Kraus-Thomson, 1982.

—————. *Writings in Periodicals Edited by W.E.B. Du Bois: Selections from "The Crisis,"* vol. 2. Millwood, N.Y.: Kraus-Thomson, 1983.

—————. *Writings in Periodicals Edited by W.E.B. Du Bois: Selections from "The Horizon."* White Plains, N.Y.: Kraus-Thomson, 1985.

ASALH (Association for the Study of African American Life and History). *The Niagara Movement: Protest Reborn.* Washington, D.C.: 2005.

Crowe, Charles. "Racial Massacre in Atlanta, September 22, 1906." *The Journal of Negro History*, April 1969, pp. 150–73.

Du Bois, W.E.B. *The Autobiography of W.E.B. Du Bois: A Soliloquy on Viewing My Life from the Last Decade of Its First Century.* Introduction by Werner Sollors. New York: Oxford University Press, 2007.

—————. *Black Folk Then and Now: An Essay in the History and Sociology of the Negro Race.* Introduction by Wilson J. Moses. New York: Oxford University Press, 2007.

—————. *Black Reconstruction in America: An Essay Toward a History of the Part Which Black Folk Played in the Attempt to Reconstruct Democracy in America 1860–1880.* Introduction by David Levering Lewis. New York: Oxford University Press, 2007.

—————. *Darkwater: Voices from Within the Veil.* Introduction by Evelyn Brooks Higginbotham. New York: Oxford University Press, 2007.

———. *Dusk of Dawn: An Essay Toward an Autobiography of a Race Concept.* Introduction by Kwame Anthony Appiah. New York: Oxford University Press, 2007.

———. "The Evolution of Negro Leadership." *Dial* magazine, July 16, 1902. Online: http://teachingamericanhistory.org.

———. *In Battle for Peace: The Story of My 83rd Birthday.* Introduction by Manning Marable. New York: Oxford University Press, 2007.

———. "Of the Training of Black Men." *Atlantic Monthly,* September 1902, pp. 290–97. Online: http://etext.virginia.edu.

———. *The Philadelphia Negro: A Social Study.* Introduction by Lawrence Bobo. New York: Oxford University Press, 2007.

———. *The Souls of Black Folk.* 1903 edition. Introduction by Arnold Rampersad. New York: Oxford University Press, 2007.

———. *The Souls of Black Folk.* 50th Anniversary edition. New York: Blue Heron Press, 1953.

———. "Strivings of the Negro People." *Atlantic Monthly,* August 1897, pp. 194–98. Online: http://etext.lib.virginia.edu.

———. *The Suppression of the African Slave-Trade to the United States of America, 1638–1870.* Introduction by Saidiya Hartman. New York: Oxford University Press, 2007.

Duster, Alfreda M., editor. *Crusade for Justice: The Autobiography of Ida B. Wells.* Chicago: University of Chicago Press, 1972.

Fisk Herald, October 1886 and December 1886.

Fox, Stephen R. *The Guardian of Boston: William Monroe Trotter.* New York: Atheneum, 1971.

Franklin, John Hope, and Alfred A. Moss, Jr. *From Slavery to Freedom: A History of Negro Americans.* 6th edition. New York: Knopf, 1988.

Graham Du Bois, Shirley. *His Day Is Marching On: A Memoir of W.E.B. Du Bois.* New York: J.B. Lippincott, 1971.

Harlan, Louis R. *Booker T. Washington: The Making of a Black Leader, 1856–1901.* New York: Oxford University Press, 1975.

———, editor. *Booker T. Washington Papers.* Online: http://www.historycooperative.org/btw.

Huggins, Nathan, editor. *W.E.B. Du Bois: Writings.* New York: Library of America, 1986.

Lewis, David Levering. *W.E.B. Du Bois: Biography of a Race, 1868–1919.* New York: John Macrae/Henry Holt, 1993.

———. *W.E.B. Du Bois: The Fight for Equality and the American Century, 1919–1963.* New York: John Macrae/Henry Holt, 2000.

———, editor. *W.E.B. Du Bois: A Reader.* New York: John McRae/Henry Holt, 1995.

Marable, Manning. *W.E.B. Du Bois: Black Radical Democrat.*

Updated edition. Boulder, Colo.: Paradigm Publishers, 2005.

Moses, Wilson Jeremiah. *Alexander Crummell: A Study of Civilization and Discontent*. Amherst: University of Massachusetts Press, 1992.

National Convention of Colored Men, at Louisville, Ky. September 24, 1883. Louisville: Courier-Journal Job Printing Co., 1883.

New York Times. "Du Bois Tells Harlem Only U.S. Wants War." October 6, 1950.

New York Times. "Text of the Acheson Statement." July 13, 1950.

Ovington, Mary White. *Black and White Sat Down Together: The Reminiscences of an NAACP Founder*. New York: The Feminist Press, 1996.

Sollors, Werner, Caldwell Titcomb, and Thomas A. Underwood, editors. *Blacks at Harvard: A Documentary History of African-American Experience at Harvard and Radcliffe*. New York: New York University Press, 1993.

Time magazine. "Tumult at the Waldorf." April 4, 1949. Online: http://time.com/time/magazine/article/0,9171,799973,00.html.

Vincent, Theodore G. *Voices of a Black Nation: Political Journalism in the Harlem Renaissance*. Trenton, N.J.: Africa World Press, 1991.

Williams, Juan. *Thurgood Marshall: American Revolutionary*. New York: Three Rivers Press, 1998.

INDEX

Note: Page numbers in *italics* refer to photographs.